Praise for
Stepping Up

'*Stepping Up* is a deeply important book that applies biblical principles to the reality of 21st-century family life. Esther draws on scripture, case studies, and her own experience of becoming a stepparent, helping readers to navigate the complex web of emotions and boundaries and find joy within blended families. Refreshingly honest, realistic, and full of warmth and wisdom, this is a book that can help all family relationships.'
Kate Nicholas, author, speaker, and preacher

'*Stepping Up* is a gentle and honest companion for those navigating the complexities of stepfamily life. Drawing on lived experience and faith, Esther Kuku offers encouragement for the journey, holding space for both the challenges and the hope.'
Chine McDonald, writer, broadcaster, and author of *Unmaking Mary: Shattering the myth of perfect motherhood*

 Ministries

15 The Chambers, Vineyard
Abingdon OX14 3FE
+44(0)1865 319700 | brf.org.uk

Bible Reading Fellowship (BRF) is a charity (233280)
and company limited by guarantee (301324),
registered in England and Wales

EU Authorised Representative: Easy Access System Europe –
Mustamäe tee 50, 10621 Tallinn, Estonia, **gpsr.requests@easproject.com**

ISBN 978 1 80039 424 7
First published 2026
10 9 8 7 6 5 4 3 2 1 0
All rights reserved

Esther Kuku

STEPPING UP

A devotional for
stepfamilies

BRF
Ministries

To my wonderful family – I love you all so much.

Thank you to my husband for your unwavering support.

Contents

FAITH AND TRUST

PRAYER AND THE HOLY SPIRIT

Introduction

No one dreams of being a stepparent, but that is where the adventure begins. For me personally, and in all likelihood for you as well if you are part of a stepfamily, it has been a roller-coaster ride. My husband and I are more in love than ever before, but it has not always been easy, and I am certain there are further challenges ahead.

People in stepfamilies often feel that they're alone. You are not. It's been 14 years since I started my stepparent journey, and I did feel very alone for the first few years. Faith rarely understands where it's being led, but it trusts the one who is leading. I got married when I was 40 and immediately became a bonus mum to two beautiful little people who were six and eight. Today they are young adults, thriving in life and finding their way, and we all love each other very much.

In this book you will find practical guidance and biblical pointers I've learnt through my own personal experience as both a stepmum and bio-mum. I've also enlisted the help of other stepparents and children who have stepparents, who share their tips and experiences. We are all in this together. Community and learning from one another is key to our success.

Stepping Up: A devotional for stepfamilies is a book packed with pearls of wisdom and encouragement, as well as a good dose of reality aimed at leading you towards peace and fulfilment. Pick it up and read it whenever you need to, and you'll be strengthened and empowered to embrace the beautiful gift of family that God has entrusted to you.

Statistics and stepfamilies

In recent years, the landscape of family structures in the United Kingdom has undergone significant change. Stepfamilies are now one of the fastest-growing family types. According to the latest data from the Office for National Statistics (ONS), in 2021 there were approximately 781,000 stepfamilies in England and Wales. Of these, 547,000 (70%) contained dependent children. This represents a notable shift from previous decades, reflecting broader societal changes and evolving family dynamics.

Stepfamilies now account for a significant portion of households with dependent children. In 2021, 8.8% (1.1 million) of dependent children lived in stepfamilies, a slight decrease from 9.7% (1.2 million) in 2011. Despite this decrease, the presence of stepfamilies remains substantial, highlighting the importance of understanding and supporting our unique family units.

The formation of stepfamilies is primarily driven by the dissolution of previous relationships, such as divorce or separation, followed by the formation of new partnerships. The increasing rate of divorce and separation in the UK has contributed to the rise in stepfamilies. According to the ONS, the divorce rate in England and Wales was 8.9 per 1,000 married men and women in 2021. This trend underscores the need for resources and support systems tailored to the specific challenges faced by our stepfamilies.

Stepfamilies often navigate complex dynamics, including blending children from previous relationships, establishing new family roles, and managing relationships with non-resident parents. These challenges can be compounded by societal expectations and the emotional adjustments required by all family members. However, with the right support and guidance, stepfamilies can thrive and create nurturing, loving environments for all involved.

As we delve into the intricacies of stepfamily life, it is essential to recognise the unique strengths and opportunities that our families bring. Through open communication, mutual respect, and a strong foundation of faith, stepfamilies can overcome obstacles and build harmonious, resilient households. *Stepping Up: A devotional for stepfamilies* aims to provide practical, faith-based guidance to help stepfamilies navigate their journey with grace and confidence.

How to use this book

This book is for stepparents and their spouse or partner. It's designed to be practical and flexible; you don't need to read it in order or follow a strict plan. Instead, it can be opened at any page at any time, allowing God to meet you right where you are.

Stepping Up: A devotional for stepfamilies is divided into 60 reflections that cover a wide range of subjects, each chosen to reflect the real challenges and blessings of stepfamily life. Woven within the devotions are first-person stepfamily stories. Whether you are navigating relationships between children and stepparents, seeking peace in your marriage, or simply needing strength for the day ahead, you can navigate to the section that speaks to your situation and find insight, encouragement, and prayer.

Every devotion is short enough to fit into busy schedules, yet deep enough to provide lasting impact. Each one also includes a 'Stepping stones' section, which contains nuggets of truth to carry into your day.

This book is meant to be a friend on the journey, a resource you can return to again and again. As you invite God into your daily life through these devotions, you will find renewed strength, fresh perspective, and the assurance that he is building something eternal through your stepfamily.

Nick and Gill's story

Nick and Gill have been together since 2017 and got married in 2020. Nick had one daughter prior to their marriage. Nick says:

Being part of a blended family has been a deeply rewarding experience. Gill has stepped into her role with compassion, patience, and a strong desire to nurture, forming a meaningful bond with my daughter that has grown through shared moments and mutual respect. She brings a fresh perspective and often plays a key role in creating a warm and stable home environment. Her efforts to support, guide, and care for my daughter are rooted in love and not obligation, which makes her role uniquely heartfelt. The presence of Gill in our lives has enriched our lives, providing additional emotional support and encouragement. She has helped to strengthen the family unit by promoting harmony, understanding, and open communication. Through dedication and kindness, we have both helped build a sense of belonging, making our family not just functional but connected and thriving.

Gill says:

Becoming a stepmother later in life has not been without its challenges, however, it is a very rewarding experience, and with communication and respect we work together as a family to address any problems that may arise.

Nick and Gill's top tips

- Communication is important
- Don't be too hard on yourself when you make mistakes
- Respect boundaries

The journey

1

Embracing brokenness

He who was seated on the throne said, 'I am making every-thing new!' Then he said, 'Write this down, for these words are trustworthy and true.'
REVELATION 21:5

In the art of kintsugi, Japanese crafters repair broken pottery with paint mixed with powdered gold, silver, or platinum. This technique highlights the cracks and imperfections rather than hiding them, creating a unique and beautiful piece of art that embraces the history of its breakage. Kintsugi teaches us that brokenness and restoration are part of an object's history, adding to its beauty and worth.

The philosophy behind the technique is built on the concept of embracing our flaws and imperfections.

As stepfamilies, you may face challenges that make you feel like your family is fragmented or imperfect. However, just like the art of kintsugi, our brokenness can be transformed into something beautiful. The Bible reminds us in 2 Corinthians 12:9: 'My grace is sufficient for you, for my power is made perfect in weakness.' Through faith, we can find strength in our vulnerabilities and imperfections.

When we accept and acknowledge the cracks in our family dynamics, we open ourselves to God's healing power. He can fill our broken places with his grace, mercy, and love, creating a masterpiece that reflects his glory.

Just as kintsugi emphasises the beauty in repaired pottery and the transformation that follows, we should celebrate the uniqueness of our families. Each member brings their own experiences, strengths, and perspectives, contributing to the richness of our family tapestry.

Stepping stones

- **We can trust in God's promise to make all things new** and allow his love to shine through the cracks in our lives.

2

Is this love?

The Spirit of the Sovereign Lord is on me,
    because the Lord has anointed me
    to proclaim good news to the poor.
He has sent me to bind up the brokenhearted,
    to proclaim freedom for the captives
    and release from darkness for the prisoners,
to proclaim the year of the Lord's favour
    and the day of vengeance of our God,
to comfort all who mourn,
    and provide for those who grieve in Zion –
to bestow on them a crown of beauty
    instead of ashes,
the oil of joy
    instead of mourning,
and a garment of praise
    instead of a spirit of despair.
They will be called oaks of righteousness,
    a planting of the Lord
    for the display of his splendour.
ISAIAH 61:1–3

I remember the morning after my wedding like it was yesterday. The plan was that my stepchildren were supposed to stay with family so my new husband and I could have a blissful first morning together as newlyweds in our honeymoon suite. Unfortunately, someone either dropped the ball or didn't get the memo; there was a loud knock on our door, and two excitable small people were presented to us.

They headed straight for the hydra bath and giggled infectiously while turning on taps. I held back the tears and smiled at my husband. We couldn't possibly have an argument on day one.

Thirteen years on, I can laugh as we look back over what God has done in our lives. He has given us beauty for ashes, the oil of joy for mourning, and the garment of praise for the spirit of heaviness. Our marriage is the planting of the Lord that he might be glorified.

There is a tightrope of hurt feelings that you will encounter many times over as a stepfamily. You must determine that you are in it for the long haul. Always remember this is what you prayed for; you love each other. Prioritise your marriage and demonstrate to your children that your relationship comes first. This is very important. If you were in a traditional marriage or relationship, you would have had time to get to know one another prior to children coming along.

Build a network of supportive people around you and agree with each other who you will talk to about your relationship. No marriage is easy, so you need to find your trusted tribe. Give each other space to get it wrong. And – this is a tough one – in the early years defer to the biological parent when it comes to their children. This will not be the right approach forever, but in the initial stages of blending your family it is.

Stepping stones

- Our destiny in life is not due to anything we have done, but because the Spirit of the Lord is upon us. **He has anointed us for good works.** It is not about us; it is all about him.

- The phrase 'blended family' is a huge misnomer. When two families come together for the first time, you are far from blended. Rather, you are a 'merging' family, and this can and will be challenging. **With time and prayer, all hearts will unite** and the God who makes everything beautiful in his time will be glorified.

3

Mergers and mercy

The steadfast love of the Lord never ceases,
    his mercies never come to an end;
they are new every morning;
    great is your faithfulness.
LAMENTATIONS 3:22–23 (NRSV)

Have you ever been in an organisation that merges with another? There are valid business reasons and clear transformational opportunities that the merger offers. Senior leaders from both sides agree and are excited by two organisations becoming one. However, the unseen power of organisational culture is often overlooked. Vision and values are defined by chief executives and leadership teams, but if the people who have to carry out the vision haven't 'bought in', then challenges ensue. In walks misunderstanding, friction, and tension. This makes it difficult for teams to work together successfully.

Sound familiar? Mum and dad are in love, and they've agreed the vision for their lives together; the only potential challenge is that vision now needs to be socialised with your key internal stakeholders – the kids!

Every intimate relationship needs a culture of love, faithfulness, and trust, especially marriage. However, in stepfamilies the process can be different. Often where you have children or family members who don't love you, you first have to commit to sacrificial giving to build trust, which can then open the door to love. This process can come with rejection, which can be discouraging and hurtful, but mercy can be the perfect tool.

Mercy sees the hurting heart and not the hurtful words, and choses grace over offence. Mercy also chooses to forgive what is unsaid, perhaps the support we'd hope to receive from our spouse, the biological parent. We can't change people and circumstances, but we can change our approach to one of peace and hope, and we can choose mercy over judgement, especially when it comes to young children who have been plunged into a situation that is not of their making. How we respond makes all the difference.

Stepping stones

- Jesus told us that when we are burdened, **we can come to him to find rest** (Matthew 11:28–30). He knows all about your pain and lovingly waits for you to bring it to him.

- **You are not alone.** Speak to a trusted friend who loves both you and your spouse. We must learn to relinquish our desire for control and trust God; through your faith he will supply all your needs and direct your paths. He is rooting for your rise and wants your stepfamily to be an example of his redemptive power. You will overcome, and other couples will be blessed by the light you carry.

4

The biblical stepfamily

Because Joseph her husband was faithful to the law, and yet did not want to expose her to public disgrace, he had in mind to divorce her quietly. But after he had considered this, an angel of the Lord appeared to him in a dream and said, 'Joseph son of David, do not be afraid to take Mary home as your wife, because what is conceived in her is from the Holy Spirit.'
MATTHEW 1:19–20

Jesus was 'conceived of the spirit and born of the virgin Mary'; Joseph was chosen by God to be stepfather to Jesus. As Matthew records, he stood by Mary even though he had initial misgivings, and we get a real glimpse into his character when we see him be faithful despite the difficulty. How great to be able to find comfort in the fact that the biblical fabric and parental identity of our Lord and Saviour is wrapped within a stepfamily context.

Joseph demonstrated profound humility and leadership. Obeying God was a priority; when the angel of the Lord appeared to him and encouraged him not to be afraid and to take Mary as his wife, he obeyed. Joseph's obedience is also on display on two other occasions. When the angel appears to Joseph and commands him to take Mary and Jesus to Egypt to protect Jesus from the hands of Herod (Matthew 2:13–14), Joseph immediately does so, saving Jesus' life. Then, after Herod dies, the angel appears once again and commands Joseph to return to Israel (Matthew 2:19), which he once again does. We see a consistent pattern of obedience and humility no matter what the situation looked like.

The very fact that Joseph had the legal right to divorce Mary when he discovered she was pregnant indicates that he was understood to not be Jesus' biological father, otherwise this option would not have been open to him. He had planned to do this discretely because he didn't want to bring shame on her, another mark of his exceptional character. Following their marriage, he didn't have sex with Mary until after the birth of Jesus: Joseph protected the validity of the virgin birth (Matthew 1:25).

We see here an important example for every stepfamily to understand. There is something unique about the hearts and minds of those God chooses to raise children who are not their own. Through his strength, we are able and more than capable. It is the greatest honour.

Stepping stones

- **Lay the difficulty and your lack of confidence before him** and, in the face of bereavement or brokenness, don't let your heart be troubled. Stop worrying about the fact that you are not the biological parent. Joseph wasn't worrying about the fact that he wasn't Jesus' 'real dad'; he still moved forward and fulfilled his purpose.

- **Be focused.** I remember, not long after I got married, someone asking me why I decided to 'take on' a ready-made family. I was shocked and didn't know what to say. Sometimes all we need to do is be still and allow God to take control when you don't understand the assignment he has for you. In time, your success will be evident, and his glory will be seen by all.

- If you're the biological parent, **pray for your spouse** and give them the space and time they need to adjust.

5

One size does not fit all...

> There are different kinds of gifts, but the same Spirit distributes them. There are different kinds of service, but the same Lord. There are different kinds of working, but in all of them and in everyone it is the same God at work.
> 1 CORINTHIANS 12:4–6

This passage emphasises that diversity within the body of Christ is intentional and valuable. Just as within the community of believers there are different gifts and services, so too each stepfamily is unique, with its own set of dynamics, strengths, and challenges that require a tailored approach.

What works for my family may not necessarily work for yours. I didn't have children when I got married; my husband did. Some couples are both bringing young children into their family unit, and others have adult children who have left home and may have wider concerns regarding their parent starting again much later in life. Similarly, the circumstances of families coming together may look different; one or both parents may have experienced bereavement. Not all stepfamilies result from divorce; some are formed when single parents with children from previous relationships come together.

Sometimes, a stepparent may need to discipline very young children directly to ensure their safety. This is generally easier with younger children. For older children, if the biological parent is present, it's best to let them take charge of discipline. Trust your instincts, guided by the relationship you have with the children. If the biological parent is not around and the children act disrespectfully, inform the biological parent later so they can address the behaviour. If you're the biological parent, handle the situation in a way that shows respect and support for your spouse as well as for your children.

Adult stepchildren may not even accept that title for themselves and not even biological parents can discipline adult children – that ship has pretty much sailed! They have lived a whole life and are not looking for new parental figures. In this instance, setting boundaries around respect is important. They may not be in your home every day, but they may see your home as their inheritance. Their behaviour may be embedded in entitlement or simply in wanting to protect their parent and everything that the family has achieved prior to your arrival.

We have to embrace the diversity within our homes and families, respecting the individual needs of each family member, even if we don't always understand the behaviour we're seeing. Believing the best in each other and looking for the positive in what is being communicated is always a healthy approach. Over time, this will bring us closer to an environment where everyone feels valued, heard, and understood.

 ## Stepping stones

- **Boundaries are essential to keeping healthy relationships with adult stepchildren** as they lay the foundation for mutual respect. Be very clear with your language when you're setting out what is acceptable and what isn't. Be consistent with boundaries, otherwise they will not be respected.

- **Actively listen** – and lead with your emotions when speaking. Don't say: 'Your behaviour towards my husband/wife is disrespectful.' Try: 'I find myself feeling disrespected and not heard sometimes when we discuss my new marriage.'

- **Aim to always be on the same page with your spouse.** This may mean planning for difficult conversations and discussing how you intend to present a united front.

6

Romance may have to wait

Let us not become weary in doing good, for at the proper time we will reap a harvest if we do not give up.
GALATIANS 6:9

The transition of knitting a stepfamily together is always complex. This is a hard thing to say, but, in all honesty, the romantic dream may have to wait a while. This comes back to putting the emotional needs of the children first. This may feel like it's in conflict with always putting your marriage first, which you should also do – but it isn't.

Intimacy and romance in marriage are vital for it to thrive. However, in the stepparent home this will only start to really flourish when your family structure is more balanced and peaceful. Plus, the trust and bond in your relationship will have a much greater depth and strength. You want your spouse to know and feel completely at peace about the relationship you have with their children. You don't want them to feel like they have to choose. Equally, a biological parent needs to support their spouse in that blending process. It may take longer if they have never had children before. The ultimate benefit of prioritising children's emotional needs will be a seriously strong marriage and secure children who feel safe in your union.

Don't rush to play happy families and paper over cracks that are clearly there. I didn't have children when we got married, so initially we were only dealing with my husband's. Your situation may be different; for example, you may both be bringing children into the new family environment. Take your time and read the room. Sit down with all the children and talk through their expectations, and make space for them to discuss how they feel. They may say very little at first, but usually if you create an environment that is conducive for sharing, at some point, and in God's time, children will share. Model the practice of patience for children; it will set a solid foundation for your home.

Stepping stones

- In Galatians, Paul urges the churches to live a life that is consistent with what they believe. **Don't grow weary of being kind** and patient and of exercising self-control. Don't get tired of demonstrating the fruit of the Spirit in your home (see Galatians 5:22–23) and of being gentle and peaceful. If you do, the work of the flesh will take over, and the outcome will not be good. Sow in the Spirit and you will reap of the Spirit; this is a principle that cannot fail.

- If you do move too quickly or just become frustrated, **ensure you have a plan** to handle the situation better next time.

- **Apologise to your spouse and your stepchildren** if you have overstepped boundaries, and find a way to put it right – don't worry too much about it.

- **Remember that patience isn't only the ability to wait but also the capacity to have a good attitude while waiting.** Pray for God's help to endure, and trust God that it won't be long before you get your romantic ending.

7

Embracing perspective

'As long as the earth endures,
seedtime and harvest,
cold and heat,
summer and winter,
day and night
will never cease.'
GENESIS 8:22

Sometimes we will need to take a step back and assess the broader landscape. While the unique dynamics of blending families can present their own set of challenges, it's important to recognise that some difficulties we face are simply part of raising children – whether they're toddlers testing boundaries or teenagers asserting their independence.

In Genesis 8:22, we are reminded of the natural cycles and seasons established by God. We can extend this concept to the regular trials and triumphs that come with parenting. It can be easy to attribute all struggles to the stepfamily setup, but sometimes we're merely navigating the universal challenges of parenthood.

Perspective is key. By acknowledging that certain difficulties are part of the regular journey, we can cut ourselves some slack. It's not always about us; sometimes it's just the age and stage of our children. Allow this realisation to bring you a sense of relief and affirmation. We're doing our best, and some of these bumps in the road are simply par for the course.

In these moments, lean into grace. Understand that every family has its highs and lows, and it's okay to feel overwhelmed. Instead of viewing every issue as a reflection of the fact that your family is different to everyone else's, embrace the idea that parenting is a complex, evolving process. Celebrate the small victories and recognise the resilience within your family.

Remember, God sees your efforts and walks alongside you. In the words of Isaiah 41:10: 'Do not fear, for I am with you; do not be dismayed, for I am your God. I will strengthen you and help you; I will uphold you with my righteous right hand.' Trust in his guidance and take comfort in knowing that you are not alone on this journey.

Stepping stones

- **In both traditional families and stepfamilies, the blessings of children are the same.** Each child is a reminder of God's goodness. They grow up so quickly and before you know it, they've left home. It is important that we cherish every moment and don't dwell on the difficulty too much. It will pass.

- **This verse highlights the blessing of children** and the importance of cherishing them, despite the challenges:

  Children are a heritage from the Lord,
      offspring a reward from him.
  PSALM 127:3

- **This verse helps us maintain a heavenly perspective**, focusing on the eternal rather than the temporary trials:

  For our light and momentary troubles are achieving for us an eternal glory that far outweighs them all. So we fix our eyes not on what is seen, but on what is unseen, since what is seen is temporary, but what is unseen is eternal.
  2 CORINTHIANS 4:17–18

8

Navigating change

There is a time for everything, and a season for every activity under the heavens.
ECCLESIASTES 3:1

Interruption and inconvenience are things we have to learn to embrace and adapt to if we are going to live emotionally intelligent lives.

Change is an inevitable part of life. It happens in our personal lives, our work, and especially within our homes. As we blend our families and navigate new relationships, the rhythm of our lives will constantly be changing. Seasons will always come and go, bringing new challenges and opportunities.

Learn to go with the flow; don't overthink everything; save your energy for the battles that count. Not every hill is worth climbing, and not every battle is worth fighting. Accepting this truth allows us to approach change not as a disruption, but rather as a natural progression.

Carefully planned change is great; for example, the summer holiday that you've planned all year. It's the didn't-plan-it, didn't-expect-it, or didn't-ask-for-it sort of change that can trigger anxiety. Perhaps someone has walked out of your life and now you are starting again. Or maybe someone has done something that has nothing to do with you and now you are suffering the consequences. This is where we lean on the sovereignty of God and trust him, even if we can't see any trace of him in what we're experiencing.

The neuroplasticity of our brains craves change – whether it's posi-tive or negative. Did you know that there are neural pathways in our brain that will die if we don't do new things? When we engage in new activities or experiences, we strengthen existing neural connections and form new ones. Conversely, if we don't challenge our brains with new experiences, some neural pathways may weaken and eventually die off. This process is known as synaptic pruning, where the brain eliminates weaker connections to make room for stronger, more efficient ones. Doing change well can enhance our emotional intelligence and resilience. It teaches us to adapt, grow, and find new strengths within ourselves. (See **dontloseyourmind.com/post/6-simple-ways-to-build-new-neural-pathways-in-your-brain**.)

Stepping stones

- **Change is both hard and healthy. It's also great for the health of our brain.** Keeping our brains positively active and engaged with new experiences is essential for maintaining cognitive health and promoting lifelong learning.

- **Try to think of something new you can do as a family at least twice a year.** A couple of years ago my husband discovered fishing, and now we all go fishing as a family during the summer. Whether we catch something is not as important as the fact that we are all together having fun.

- **When you are facing change that you didn't ask for, focus on gratitude** and what you have gained instead of what you have lost. Establish new rhythms, connect with new people, and start to build new memories that will in time result in fresh enthusiasm.

- **God's help is available to help us** navigate unanticipated adjustments if we're willing to accept it.

- **When we're learning to adjust, not everything is a priority.** If we put God first, he will help us to prioritise everything else.

Emily's story

Emily was 20 when her stepdad entered her life. Following a turbulent marriage, her mum left her father. As a newly formed single-parent family, Emily, her sister, and her mother were all very close. However, six months later, her mum met someone and it was not long after that she remarried. The quickness was a challenge; it felt too soon for Emily and her sister, who was 17. Their new stepdad was in his 50s and had never had children himself or been married before. They were young adults and didn't need his input. Emily, now 34, says:

> I was doing my A levels and about to go university. I would have preferred it if he did have a family of his own, because it just felt like he was uncomfortable around us – he preferred his own company, as he'd done so much life alone. I mentioned this to my mum, and she rightly said that then we would have had stepsiblings, and our new normal would have been even more complex to navigate. He tried to parent us, but we were resistant. For so many years our mum had been both mum and dad; she was everything to us.
>
> It's taken 14 years to figure out what the relationship looks like, and honestly we're still figuring it out now. In the early days it did feel like someone was coming in and taking Mum's time and attention. Today, we have found a rhythm whereby he doesn't try to parent us, and he comes to big social events, but we don't see him that much. We have established a routine and are getting better at sharing Mum. Though it's still a process, our situation has improved significantly. We know that she is cared for and looked after, and we can still do life with her, but it just looks a bit different.

It's been a journey. I've had therapy and lots of prayer. My sister and I are very close, and we've supported each other throughout but, even though years have gone by, it still feels quite hard. Now I'm a mum myself, I have a bit more understanding of the importance of her happiness. I appreciate that life has seasons, and my mum deserves to have someone to take care of her. My stepdad can do that. So, although there was definitely jealousy right at the beginning, it has eased. Now my sister and I are both married and have our own homes. It does become easier with time.

Having a neutral sounding board and someone to talk to in terms of therapy was invaluable. For example, we've had high expectations of our mum that sometimes she can't meet, and we've been learning to understand what the reasons are. It's been useful, via counselling, to talk through boundaries and expectations. Everyone should go to therapy, whether you feel that you need it or not, to get perspective and have that neutral person to help you untangle things. It's a constant journey; I've learnt to be honest and vulnerable and put God first. He will be with us as we work through the new seasons, even when you're clinging on with your fingernails.

Emily's top tips

- **Talk about how you're feeling** as much as you possibly can, instead of stewing in worry.

- **Try to find interests that you can all do together.** In our lives, the only thing that connects us is Mum, so we will go for a walk and a pub lunch. Even if you're very young, or adults, find things you can do together even if it's a movie night.

- **Journalling can be good** to brain dump and pour out your feelings.

- **Find a way to keep God front and centre** as he is the one that will restore and redeem and bring you through the good and the bad.

- **It's important to remember that we've never been stepchildren before,** and they've never been stepparents before. Everyone is trying to work out what the new seasons looks like.

- **Our earthly parents or stepparents may not get everything right,** but God's love is perfect.

- **Remember every family has dysfunction** when you look a bit closer beneath the surface. Every one of us is going through something and there is always so much to bond over. Ask God to help you to find like-minded people.

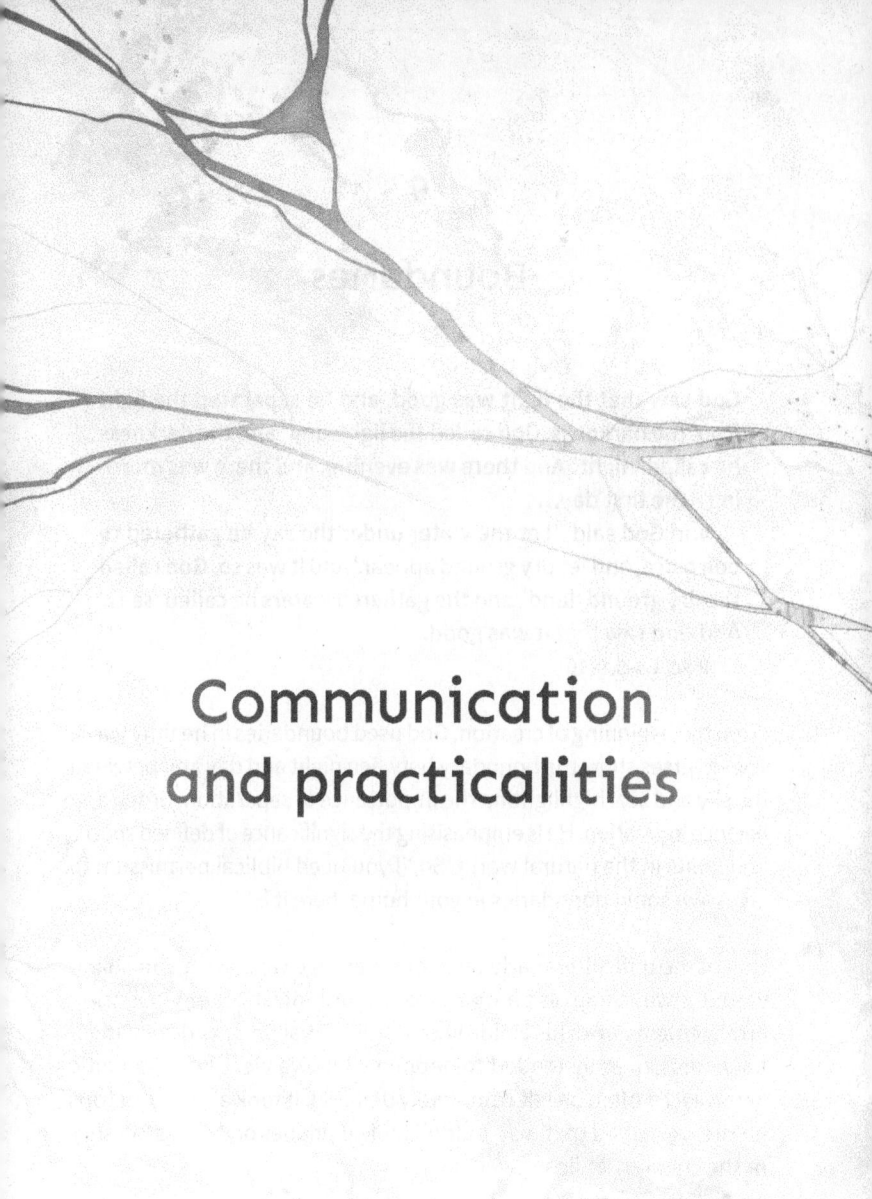

Communication
and practicalities

9

Boundaries

God saw that the light was good, and he separated the light from the darkness. God called the light 'day', and the darkness he called 'night'. And there was evening, and there was morning – the first day…

And God said, 'Let the water under the sky be gathered to one place, and let dry ground appear.' And it was so. God called the dry ground 'land', and the gathered waters he called 'seas.' And God saw that it was good.

GENESIS 1:4–5, 9–10

From the beginning of creation, God used boundaries in healthy ways. These verses show the boundary between night and day and between the sky and sea, highlighting the importance of separation, order, and balance in creation. He is emphasising the significance of defined spaces and limits in the natural world. So, if you need biblical permission to lay down some boundaries in your home, here it is!

One of the difficulties early on in our marriage was that my husband would always address a message around logistics and visitation arrangements from his children's mother in real time, and coincidentally, this generally tended to happen while we were on a romantic getaway! I'd often be left completely deflated. It took a couple of trips before we agreed that we wouldn't look at phones or discuss logistics or the children while we were away.

These scenarios, however, would never happen in a traditional family. They are unique to stepfamilies, and it's another reason why putting in place clear boundaries are important.

When consistently applied, they will ensure that everyone's needs and feelings are considered and can help build healthy relationships between new couples and ex-partners. In turn, this will reduce the possibility for conflict and misunderstandings and help foster cooperative co-parenting.

Boundaries will help the stability in your home and empower you to have an honest conversation with each other about how you see co-parenting working. When will you take calls from an ex-partner and when will you not? What constitutes an emergency and what doesn't? How involved will the stepparent be? In some cases, stepparents and the ex-partner of a bio-parent may get on well. In other scenarios, you may agree to stick to the bio-parent consistently taking the lead. The most important thing is that you talk it through.

Boundaries are a divine principle established from the beginning of creation, promoting order and balance: set them.

Stepping stones

- **Boundaries will prevent conflicts** that might arise from past relationships interfering with new ones. They are about what is okay and what is not okay, and setting them is not unkind; it is healthy.

- **It is not okay to keep having the same conversation** about problematic behaviour that is having a negative influence on a new relationship. Setting boundaries will help with this.

- **Saying no is okay.** 'No' is a sentence.

- **An example conversation about boundaries** with your partner or spouse: 'It is very important that we all have a good co-parenting relationship. What does that look like for you? And can we think how we do this in a way that considers everyone's feelings.'

- Many times, we talk about not being led by our emotions, but in stepfamilies it's important that couples **have a clear understanding of how each one of you feels** and not to assume one another's emotions.

- The following verse refers to the creation narrative and underscores **the permanence and necessity of boundaries:**

  'Should you not fear me?' declares the Lord. 'Should you not tremble in my presence? I made the sand a boundary for the sea, an everlasting barrier it cannot cross. The waves may roll, but they cannot prevail; they may roar, but they cannot cross it.'
  JEREMIAH 5:22

10

The blending blind spot

By wisdom a house is built,
    and through understanding it is established.
PROVERBS 24:3

This verse emphasises the importance of wisdom and understanding in establishing a strong and stable home. Blending families is a beautiful yet complex journey, often accompanied by unexpected challenges. Every stepparent will be aware of what I'm going to call 'the blending blind spot' that can occur and cause tension between biological parents and stepparents.

In stepfamilies, biological parents tend to be overjoyed to have their children with them, especially if visitation is limited to set times. This joy can sometimes create a blind spot, where they may not see the subtle signs of disrespect or tension between their children and their spouse. The stepparent, being less emotionally embedded, may notice behaviours and attitudes that the biological parent doesn't see or, worse, overlooks.

Children, including adult children, in new stepfamilies might test boundaries and express their confusion or discomfort through subtle disrespect towards the stepparent. The biological parent's focus on reconnecting with their children may lead them to miss these cues.

Open communication is key for stability. If you're the stepparent, you should lovingly share your observations with your spouse. In return, it is important for biological parents to follow through on addressing inappropriate behaviour. Silence is not an option if you want to place value on your new relationship.

Working together, you can develop strategies to build respect and understanding within your family. Establishing clear boundaries and setting consistent expectations for behaviour is a crucial plan to put in place. By being attentive and proactive and deploying practical steps, you can navigate these challenges and build a harmonious, loving home. Do not ignore issues; they will just grow.

God's wisdom and guidance are our greatest tools in blending families. You've got this!

 ## Stepping stones

- **Whether children are adults or not, they may not automatically buy in to the new family unit.** Couples need to join forces and be on the same page in terms of handling disrespectful behaviour.

- **Remember the traditional family playbook is completely redundant in stepfamilies.** Children draw deep-seated strength and security from parents who love each other in a traditional home. However, in a stepfamily everything is skewed and children, of any age, can hate the fact that their parent is in love with someone new.

- **Understand that things will not change overnight**, and don't be discouraged. Maintain unity and consistency. The biological parent should continue to actively affirm their spouse in the presence of their children.

- **Children, young and old, need to know** that rudeness will not be tolerated.

11

Stepfathers and leadership

Submit to one another out of reverence for Christ. Wives, submit yourselves to your own husbands as you do to the Lord. For the husband is the head of the wife as Christ is the head of the church, his body, of which he is the Saviour.
EPHESIANS 5:21-23

According to the most recent census, most stepfamilies in the UK are formed of a biological mother and stepfather. This makes the role of stepfathers especially significant.

Scripture reminds us of the value of leadership in homes. This is not just about delegation of responsibilities; it's also about creating a cohesive and respectful family dynamic that honours biblical principles.

Ephesians 5:23 emphasises the role of the husband as a leader and a guide. It is not about control; it's about modelling Christlike humility and fostering unity. It's a tricky old verse for many, even in traditional family homes. However, every team needs a captain, and this principle extends to stepfathers as well.

Stepfathers should be recognised as a full participant in family life – not merely as someone who provides financially, but also for the care and commitment they show. Biological parents can help by affirming their spouse's role, while also discerning the appropriate pace for sharing responsibilities. Initially it is right for the biological parent to lead on discipline while blending is taking place. There should, however, be a timeframe for this that allows for both parents to jointly discipline. This is not about diminishing anyone's role; rather it is about complementing one another so you can build stronger bonds and present a united front always. Children learn respect and unity when they see adults working together in love.

Proverbs 22:6 reminds us: 'Train up a child in the way he should go; even when he is old, he will not depart from it' (ESV). Guiding children in blended families means showing them that leadership is shared, respectful, and rooted in God's wisdom.

This biblical leadership approach is vital for cultivating respect. Your children will learn to see their stepfather as a trusted authority figure and role model. It also acknowledges the commitment it takes for a man to step into a fatherly role, demonstrating his dedication and love for his spouse and her children.

Stepping stones

- **Embracing these biblical principles** not only strengthens the peace and togetherness within the home but also builds a foundation of mutual respect and love that can withstand the test of time.

- **Men who step up, step in, and become that father figure over a family are to be celebrated.** It is vital that we value them and ensure they are supported and encouraged.

- **Affirm your spouse** in front of your children.

- **Both adults should be aware of control,** we don't want to have controlling behaviour in our homes, sometimes we don't know we're doing it and it comes from a place of fear.

- **Stepdad: your spouse may be oblivious to their behaviour** as they've spent so long running things on their own. If you're struggling in this area, seek professional counselling together.

12

Money, money, money...

**The plans of the diligent lead to profit
as surely as haste leads to poverty.**
PROVERBS 21:5

Money can be one of the main things that causes strife in a home. In stepfamilies, financial harmony can be complex to achieve, but it is crucial for nurturing unity and fairness.

Proverbs 3:9–10 reminds us to honour God with our wealth, which translates to managing our finances with integrity, wisdom, and love. As stepfamilies come together, you will bring diverse sources of income – from parents, stepparents, and even extended family members like grandparents. One of you may have multiple properties, or years of investment prior to getting married, for example.

It's important that the approach is tailored to your reality. Consider making financial decisions based on the following principles.

- **Transparency:** Be open about financial contributions and decisions. This builds trust and reduces misunderstandings. If you want to leave a property in trust for your biological children, be clear about this. Think about the language you use when you're having this discussion.

- **Fairness:** Strive for equality in financial support, especially during special occasions. This helps all children feel equally loved and appreciated. Be careful of optics, particularly with young children. Don't buy your biological children all the latest gadgetry and clothing and leave your stepchildren out. Be fair.

- **Wisdom:** Seek God's guidance in financial matters. Pray together and make decisions that honour God. If you're not at the point where you can pray about these things, don't worry – many people are not. Just be wise and fair. Reassure adult children that you're not after their inheritance and that you're committed to what is best for your family.

- **Compassion:** Understand that each spouse's financial situation may differ. Show empathy and support one another. If you're married to someone who has been divorced, they might have lost a lot during that process and will feel very vulnerable and sensitive around having to start from scratch. If you're in a great job and experiencing financial success, don't splash the cash; it will make a person who has lost everything prior to meeting you feel uncomfortable. Showing compassion is key, as well as support to your spouse.

Stepping stones

- **During festive times, like Christmas, it's essential to strive for fairness,** especially with younger children who may not fully understand the complexities of stepfamily finances.

- **One practical approach is to create savings accounts for all children,** ensuring that each child feels valued and receives a fair share. Wider family members can then also contribute directly to bank accounts.

- **While biological parents and grandparents may naturally contribute more to their own children,** it is important to maintain transparency and open communication about financial decisions.

13

What's the plan?

> 'Write the vision
> And make *it* plain on tablets
> That he may run who reads it.
> For the vision *is* yet for an appointed time;
> But at the end it will speak, and it will not lie.
> Though it tarries, wait for it;
> Because it will surely come.'
>
> HABAKKUK 2:2–3 (NKJV)

A vision statement in a business will define purpose and outline standards that staff will need to align with if they are to succeed. It may feel like a bit of a stretch, but the same corporate principle can be applied to your home. Culture eats strategy – so if we don't plan for good culture in our homes, that strategy of peace and order we all desire will not stand a chance.

Have a plan for each day; do not leave things to chance. Write the vision down daily, not just at the start of the New Year. Create a vision statement for your family and put it somewhere visible, not locked away in a drawer, because we move towards what we can consistently see.

So, what goes in your vision statement? There is a well-known quote: 'People don't plan to fail; they fail to plan.' Write out some simple plans, such as: loving the way you want to be loved; serving one another unselfishly every day; giving and expecting nothing in return; being positive and not making excuses; and not being too hard on yourself. We all make mistakes; we get things wrong. Take the gift of experience that life's ups and down bring and plan, as a family, to bounce back quickly!

Be intentional in your vision statement about taking practical steps to live the abundant life that God has promised us all. His word says he has given you everything that pertains to life and godliness. We can be assured that there is nothing that we need to be successful in our homes that God has not already provided or will provide for us.

His grace is sufficient for you to maximise every opportunity available to extend yourself. Embrace his vision for your life, and make your contribution to the world.

 ## Stepping stones

Ultimately, God's word will provide us with a blueprint for the vision we want to write for our stepfamilies.

- **It's important that we sit down with our children and teach them the values and vision for our home.**

- **For children born into a family, this will be easier and almost come naturally,** even if they can't articulate it. For children who become part of a new stepfamily, it will be much harder, and will need to be simple and gently implemented.

- **Keep your statement to no more than five practical points** and remember you will not get it right all the time – it's a guide.

Sample family vision statement

We commit to creating a loving family environment every day and to allow biblical principles and the teachings of Jesus Christ to guide our heart's actions. Praying daily and rooted in our faith, we will be kind to each other even when we disagree.

We commit to being mindful of timing when discussing difficult issues and to be aware of our tone of voice. Right time, right tone. When we can't see eye to eye and disagreement and conflict sets in, we will be quick to forgive and take our challenges to God in prayer as well as agreed people we can trust.

We will embody the virtues of patience and unwavering support, nurturing a home where peace and harmony flourish, where each member of our family feels valued, loved, and empowered.

We will do our best to dedicate regular time for prayer and family devotion in order to strengthen our faith and keep Christ at the centre of our home.

> Do not be anxious about anything, but in every situation, by prayer and petition, with thanksgiving, present your requests to God. And the peace of God, which transcends all understanding, will guard your hearts and your minds in Christ Jesus.
> PHILIPPIANS 4:6-7

14

Plan for trials

Dear friends, do not be surprised at the fiery ordeal that has come on you to test you, as though something strange were happening to you. But rejoice Inasmuch as you participate in the sufferings of Christ, so that you may be overjoyed when his glory is revealed.
1 PETER 4:12–13

Tough times are a part of life, so it's a good idea to plan for them. Every marriage or relationship has its trials. It's only a matter of time before you all fall out or make mistakes in your stepparent journey. Plan for it, so you can navigate complexity with wisdom.

In an interview, Richard Willams, the father of tennis champions Serena and Venus Williams, said that he taught his daughters to prepare for losing so they were gracious in defeat. He wanted his girls to be prepared for any outcome. Richard meticulously planned the pathway to success through tennis for his girls before they were even born.

You too can plan for success by planning how you're going to handle each challenge as it comes along, even the sudden challenges that come out of nowhere – for example, when you have something exciting planned for your family on the weekend you have your stepchildren, but then the biological parent sends a list of alternative activities that the children need to do on that weekend.

Plan to focus on the positive and decide, as early on in your step-parent journey as possible, that you will not give your energy to things you can't change. Don't try to enforce rules that neither parent is going to get on board with. I remember asking my husband to set up a WhatsApp group for him, his ex-wife, and me so we could all access plans for the children. She had no intention of supporting this and left that group immediately. Remember, plan to do what will work in terms of maintaining the peace in your home as well as your own peace of mind and sanity. Anything else is not worth the negativity in your home or the battle.

Trials may come to test you, but plan to pass those tests with flying colours. And when you don't, plan to not worry about it, as there is always the next time to try again. Plan to look after yourself.

Stepping stones

- Take a back seat when you have ideas that are not in sync with the biological parents; it will just make your life easier.

- If your stepchildren spend time in another home, remember that you cannot control what goes on there – so don't worry about it. Their parents will parent as they see fit; it is not your concern. Unless there is a child safety issue, mind your own business. In the same way, the other parent has no control over how you decide to parent in your home. Simple.

- If you're a loving and supportive stepparent, your mind will wonder what is happening in the other home – that's natural when you care. But don't park up and stay there; let it go. Plan, in advance, to focus only on what you can control.

15

Reaction vs response

**The heart of the righteous weighs its answers,
but the mouth of the wicked gushes evil.**
PROVERBS 15:28

Our words are containers that carry our faith. What we say has an impact either for good or bad on the world around us. This is why it's so important to put space between how we feel and what we say.

When I got married, I moved into the home my husband had lived in with his ex-wife. Nothing about that house looked like me; everything was completely 'off brand Esther'. I complained often and felt justified to do so. Did it change the situation? No. Did it put pressure on my new husband and my young marriage? Yes. Over time I learnt to be patient, and this is still a journey.

I've also learnt to understand that the concept of emotional bookends can be a secret weapon in helping us all to make better decisions and have better conversations. Stop and think, what emotion am I feeling right now? Am I cross, exhausted? Then, think about how you want to feel on the other side of the conversation when you're looking back. Is that peace or a level of contentment?

Acknowledging how we feel will help us take better ownership of our decisions, without letting our emotions drive them. A gentle answer will defuse wrath most of the time. Harsh words, even if we don't recognise them as such in the moment, will trigger anger. Remember: intentions don't remove impact.

There are so many things we can't control. We can't, for example, control the behaviour of an ex-spouse or the legal visiting agreements put in place long before we came on the scene. But we can control how we show up. We can decide to slow down and use the right tone at the right time.

Stepping stones

- **Pray for the words you speak:** *Heavenly Father, I thank you, that your word does not return void; and therefore, my words spoken in line with your word will always accomplish what they set out to do. I want my words to progress the journey of blending and unity in our home. Thank you for empowering me with the ability to choose the right words. Help me to eliminate all idle words in my life and only speak those things that I desire to come to pass. I thank you for the result of peace and joy in my home.*

- **Our mouths can speak life or death over our future.** We have to think about not only what goes into our mouths, but also what comes out of them. A couple of years ago, I noticed that every time someone asked me how I was, I used to say I was tired. That may well have been the truth, but today if you ask me how I am, I think carefully about my answer, and make sure the words I say are helping and not hindering me.

- **Remember to always speak in the direction that you want your life to take.**

16

Permission to be angry

'In your anger do not sin': do not let the sun go down while you're still angry.
EPHESIANS 4:26

I love that God knows that situations will come along that will make us cross – and that anger is a valid response. However, we cannot allow our anger to become destructive and to transition into sin. God's standard is always the best vantage point, though you may not always resolve a situation in your home by the end of the day! Let's be real, sometimes sleeping on things and cooling down works.

Remember: once those words come out of your mouth, you can't put them back in. What you can do is settle the matter in your heart and make peace with it before you sleep. I'm continually amazed by the work of the Holy Spirit. Much better than waking up with a serious headache because you've gone to bed fuming, reserving your sleep for refreshing renewal allows room for him to speak to you.

James (1:19) tells us to be 'quick to listen, slow to speak and slow to become angry', because our anger doesn't produce the righteousness that God desires. James' letter continues with encouraging us to ditch all the malice and to humbly accept the seed of the word of God that is planted within us and has the power to save us. This is a great template for our stepfamily homes.

As a senior PR professional, words are what I work with every day. I have lots of them, and I know how to wield and unleash pithy one-liners that can cut through in whatever way I choose. It's an area of tremendous skill that can be a brilliant strength, but it is also a weakness. I remember the day my husband said to me: 'You're very calm when you speak, but it doesn't mean that what you say isn't hurtful.' I heard him clearly; he stopped me in my tracks, and I now work on being slow to speak. I never shout, at least not at my husband; my children might give you a different version of who I am (which is still a work in progress). But I have learnt not to speak to my husband if I know it is going to be challenging for me to use words that are full of grace in that moment.

Stepping stones

- **We are all human, and our heavenly Father always meets us where we are.** Take your frustration and anger and place it in his hands.

- **We can be totally honest with God.** Tell him you're finding it hard to forgive, or that you're struggling to connect with your children (biological or stepchildren) or your spouse.

- **Be kind to yourself as you continue to grow in grace.** It's okay if you get it wrong. If you're finding it difficult to pray, just worship him. And, if you're finding it hard to worship, listen to a good word-based video or podcast or speak to a trusted friend and ask them to pray for you.

- **Do whatever is godly and necessary to prevent your anger from turning into sin**, as this will only lead to stress and impact on your mental health and physical well-being.

17

Language matters

Let your conversation be always full of grace, seasoned with salt, so that you may know how to answer everyone.
COLOSSIANS 4:6

Throughout history, salt has been used as a preservative and has countless other uses, from preserving meat to taking my favourite chocolate bar to a whole new level in flavour. Throughout the Bible, salt is referred to repeatedly: it was required in sacrifices (Leviticus 2:13), used to ruin land (Deuteronomy 29:23), and used by Jesus as a metaphor for how our lives should stand out (Matthew 5:13).

When we're on that journey of managing our emotions, sometimes silence is the best answer we can give. Why? Because what is in our hearts will come out of our mouths. This is why we need to be full of the word of God, so when we speak our words will flow with grace and bring life and healing. The Bible tells us that the word of God is living, active, full of power, and sharper than any two-edged sword. It penetrates to the deepest parts of our nature, exposing and transforming our hearts (Hebrews 4:12).

A two-edged sword is a large, powerful, sharp instrument with the ability to make a tremendous impact. Today, opinion is elevated, and debates more polarised than ever. Our Bibles are our swords that can cut down judgement and opinion. Daily studying and memorising scripture will make it difficult to say the wrong thing or the right thing at the wrong time. Reading the word will allow our language to become seasoned with just the right amount of salt. This will affect our tone, so our conversations become redeeming as we learn to meet the people we care most about where they are, as opposed to where we want them to be. In this place, we model Jesus to the world around us.

Stepping stones

- **Plan a daily rhythm for reading your Bible that works for you.** Times have changed, and there are now so many innovative ways that we can all saturate ourselves in the word of God, such as by watching short videos or listening to podcasts.

- **Find a good Bible study series on YouTube and subscribe to it**, or get friends together and start a Bible study fellowship.

- **God hasn't left us to figure out life on our own;** he has given us his word to lead and guide us. And as we allow him to speak to us and through us, we will start to build a sensitivity to the people in our lives and instinctively know the approach we should take. This is vital in a home with so many competing personalities when you are on that journey of blending.

Kemi and Michael's story

Kemi, 45, didn't have any biological children when she got married and suddenly became a mother to four children. She was keen to have another child; however, her husband's enthusiasm for one more child wasn't there. Kemi struggled with feelings of desperately wanting her own biological child, while embracing her new stepfamily. It was tough.

She loved her husband deeply, but wasn't prepared to feel like the stranger in the family who invaded everyone's space. Her youngest stepchild was 15, so there was no moulding that she could do; her stepchildren were fully developed and still struggling with the death of their mother.

They would often do things to cause friction in the home, such as intentionally leaving the house in a mess after she had tidied it and refusing to eat the food Kemi had cooked. They were not interested in embracing her. Even though three of her stepchildren were young adults, much of the behaviour was deliberate.

Michael was often away, and while she longed to have a close relationship with his daughter, she just pushed her away.

On one occasion, her stepdaughter completely trashed the kitchen after cooking and left it for her to tidy. Kemi didn't do it and called her husband. The next morning, it was immaculate. But Michael had cleaned it up himself; she was furious that he hadn't made his daughter clean up after herself.

The issues were eroding her prayer life and intimacy within their marriage. It was far from the dream Kemi believed God had promised her. The most challenging thing was that Michael was a pastor, so Kemi worried about who she could confide in.

Finally, she sought counsel in a close friend and her mother. She began to realise that she was sweating the small stuff and wasn't praying into the situation. Looking back years later, she realised that she had hang-ups of her own that she had brought into the relationship and the chaos of the stepfamily dynamic just made everything worse.

> I was prioritising the wrong things and trying to build the perfect house rather than making my house a home. My focus was on ensuring that my stepchildren were falling in line rather than taking the time to develop the relationship. I was, understandably, holding grudges. Not feeling supported by my husband and being alienated by his children was deeply upsetting, but God turned it around.

They have been married for 16 years, and Kemi is now a grandma to her stepchildren's children. New babies have been the glue in the relationship between her and her stepchildren, and restoration and redemption have taken place in their home.

Kemi's top tips

- **If I was doing this all over again, I'd pray more**, and I'd prioritise building a relationship with my stepchildren.

- **I'd think about the hidden hurt that was driving their behaviour**, rather than the behaviour itself. These were primarily adult children who had lost their mother. The last thing they wanted was someone, they perceived, taking her place. I started drama where I could have been more patient.

- **God is faithful and has turned things around for our good.** There came a turning point where I said no more – no more principalities and powers trying to rule in my home. And then slowly but surely, the atmosphere changed and God started to bring beauty from ashes. If he can do that for me, he can do it for others.

Faith and trust

18

Overwhelmed

'Love the Lord your God with all your heart and with all your soul and with all your mind… Love your neighbour as yourself.'
MATTHEW 22:37, 39

Overwhelm is likely to be a new stepparent's most regular feeling. Immediate responsibility, frequent chaos, too much stuff to figure out, too much insecurity, and far too many of the emotions of others to contend with. You start to ask yourself: 'Did I hear God after all? What have I done?' Those feelings are perfectly normal.

I would constantly forget when all the times of my stepchildren's weekend activities were and even forget that it was our weekend. Then, there was the judgement from my husband for not remembering. Looking back, we were both so new at it all we didn't know how to communicate well. For me, there just seemed like so many rules. They are not allowed to eat this and not allowed to eat that. Then there was the rush to ensure dinner was done and dusted in good time prior to their bio-mum returning to collect them.

The pressure to please everyone – and also play peacekeeper – felt insurmountable, until I embraced the reality that ultimately my role is to parent and serve God with all my heart. If I serve him, he will take care of our family. Being 'liked' by everyone in the stepfamily equation isn't the goal. (You will exhaust yourself by trying to do this.) Doing our best to model godliness and be responsible adults is.

One thing I did make clear early on was that I wasn't trying to be anyone's mum. I did lay that out plain, and it helped. The words 'You are not my mum' have never been unleashed in our home. If that's something you are dealing with as you're reading this, nip it in the bud by agreeing: 'Yes, you're right, I'm not your biological parent and you don't have to like me, that's fine. But you will respect me.' Leave it at that.

Stepping stones

- **Focus on what you can control.** You can't control the remote negative engineering of an ex-spouse, or the background briefing the biological parent may be giving to your stepchildren prior to them arriving at your home. All of that is a distraction; ignore it.

- **You will not always get this right; it's a journey, so be kind to yourself.** Your spouse's ex-partner's issues are not your problem; they are a distraction.

- **Every day we make choices about how we spend our energy.** Ensure you are spending yours in the way that best serves you, loving and serving God and seeking his wisdom for building and, where it's needed, healing your home.

19

'Those he calls, he qualifies'

'For if you remain silent at this time, relief and deliverance for the Jews will arise from another place, but you and your father's family will perish. And who knows but that you have come to your royal position for such a time as this?'
ESTHER 4:14

Ever woken up and thought, *I can't do this*? Well, you can. I think about the little lives that God has allowed me to quietly influence. I see my stepchildren flourishing in life and growing into beautiful adults with their own dreams and desires. I hear them talking about marriage and get excited that, after all they've been through, marriage is still an aspiration for them. At that point, I realise that I'm grateful for the unique family that God has entrusted to me.

But God chose the foolish things of the world to shame the wise; God chose the weak things of the world to shame the strong. God chose the lowly things of this world and the despised things – and the things that are not – to nullify the things that are, so that no one may boast before him.
1 CORINTHIANS 1:27–29

You have been chosen for the family you are in; God has called you for such a time as this. Esther had been prepared physically to become queen; however, God had also prepared her to the point that he could trust her to ensure the deliverance of his people.

One of the key things we need to know when we are following the purposes of God is when to exert influence. Esther strategically prepared herself through fasting and prayer. With wisdom and humility, she approached the king and found favour in his eyes.

There will be a turning point in your marriage. One day you will wake up and you will no longer be operating from a place of pain. Doors of opportunity for a deeper relationship and a peaceful place emerge, because of the seeds of prayer and patience you've sown. It might even be now as you are reading this. God has been preparing you to be a stepparent through every mountain and valley you have overcome to this point. He is calling you out of feelings of inadequacy. It's time to arise and take your place. He has anointed you to heal, and through you he will deliver and make everything beautiful in his time. You can do all things through Christ who strengthens you (see Philippians 4:13).

Stepping stones

- **Let the world know that you're proud of your unique family unit.** We move towards what we can consistently see, so see your family as a sign and a wonder and an example to other families. Be thankful for what you've achieved together.

- **Through the resurrection power that characterises your marriage and home, God is making you broken bread and poured out wine**; you will feed and nourish others.

- **A good marriage is never perfect**, but at its core are two people who refuse to give up.

- **Don't cast away your confidence**; our boldness in Christ brings great rewards. Keep believing, be excited, and hang on tight. Your breakthrough is just around the corner.

20

Seeing Jesus in our families

He replied, 'Whether he is a sinner or not, I don't know. One thing I do know. I was blind but now I see!'
JOHN 9:25

Being a Christian and seeing Jesus are not the same thing. Many people who have never experienced Jesus have received and share in God's grace. But once you have seen him, you can never be the same. Other pastimes, habits, or behaviours will lose their appeal in the light of his glory and grace.

Separate and understand the difference between what you've seen Jesus do for you and who he really is. If you can only see what he has done for you, you are missing out and haven't really seen his sovereignty and witnessed the greatness of his power.

Stepfamilies can have the ability to allow us to see God and show off his ability to heal, deliver, and move forward in a way that can really speak into to the lives of others.

The man who was blind from birth did not know who Jesus was until he appeared and revealed himself to him. Jesus will reveal himself to your family, not necessarily in your timeframe. Make it a prayer point that he would open the eyes of your heart that you might see him, high and lifted up in all that concerns your family. That you would see what he has already done and what he will continue to do.

Just as the blind man's life was transformed through an encounter with Jesus, have faith that God will bring positive change, healing, and breakthrough within your home. Believe that affliction will not arise a second time.

Jesus accepted the blind man despite societal judgements. We can all learn to love one another, being respectful and accepting, despite past experiences. When the eyes of our understanding are enlightened, we can see clearly and are able to create supportive and inclusive family atmospheres.

The blind man's healing was a part of God's plan, reminding us to trust in his timing, even when circumstances seem difficult or uncertain. When we do see the miraculous healing hand of God in our homes, it's important that we share our testimony, as this will help to encourage others who are on a similar journey.

Stepping stones

- **Have patience and compassion.** Jesus showed compassion and patience in healing the blind man. Stepfamily members can practise patience and compassion with each other, understanding that everyone is on their unique journey of growth.

- **Share your wins.** Sharing personal experiences of faith and transformation, much like the blind man's testimony, can strengthen family relationships. It encourages openness, honesty, and mutual support.

- **You are not alone** on your stepparenting journey. Opening up and being honest about the hard bits, the rewards, and breakthroughs you experience, will be super helpful for others who are on a similar path.

21

Finding your tribe

And let us consider how we may spur one another on towards love and good deeds, not giving up meeting together, as some are in the habit of doing, but encouraging one another – and all the more as you see the Day approaching.
HEBREWS 10:24–25

Support networks are important in marriage, and even more so when you're marrying into a pre-existing family. Having a network of friends, family members, or even professionals can provide a safe space to share feelings and get advice. One of the best things that happened to me was being connected with other stepfamilies who were experiencing similar challenges, plus others who were more advanced in their marriage who helped me to see that complex situations in my family could be successfully navigated and were not unique to us.

Isolation is never a good idea – the enemy loves that! He wants to make you feel like you're alone and the only one going through that trial. He is a liar! Don't believe the lie. Community is the key to creating bonds based on common understanding.

One of my friends isn't married, but she is a sensible head, and I know that if I speak to her about my marriage – even though she was my friend first – she will never take sides! Quite often I go to her to have a whinge about my husband, and she always ends up making me see the value in his viewpoint.

Having a trusted network will improve your overall mental health and well-being and reduce stress and anxiety. Do not do life in isolation; have joint mutual friends that you do things together with, and then have individual friends that you both go off and do things separately with – that's healthy. Then, when you come back together, you have good experiences to share, and things to talk about that are not purely transactional.

Scriptures that remind us to stay connected to community:

Two are better than one,
    because they have a good return for their labour:
if either of them falls down,
    one can help the other up.
But pity anyone who falls
    and has no one to help them up.
ECCLESIASTES 4:9–10

Carry each other's burdens, and in this way you will fulfil the law of Christ.
GALATIANS 6:2

As iron sharpens iron,
    so one person sharpens another.
PROVERBS 27:17

Stepping stones

- **Conflict resolution.** Support networks can help mediate conflicts between you. And it doesn't always need to be someone who is themselves part of a stepfamily. Whether through formal counselling or informal advice, they can offer perspective and strategies for resolving disputes.

- **Good friends, who can be trusted,** can provide a neutral perspective and help you to reconcile. These are people rooting for your rise. If you don't feel you have these people in your lives, pray for God to provide them, as God always provides for all of our needs. You are fully equipped with all you need to be successful in your marriage.

22

Fear

So do not fear, for I am with you;
   do not be dismayed, for I am your God.
I will strengthen you and help you;
   I will uphold you with my righteous right hand.
ISAIAH 41:10

Fear can arise from uncertainty, feelings of inadequacy, or the practical reality of launching into the deep unknown. Members of your family may fear rejection, not being accepted, or the future dynamics of relationships. Our first job is to recognise where fear can arise and how it may present itself and then to try our best to address it with wisdom and compassion.

If you go from being two independent single-parent families to suddenly a big family unit with multiple children, that is a significant financial shift that can lead to fear concerning financial stability. Create a budget and a financial plan to address these concerns.

Embed a sense of security and open communication in your family. If you're in the process of merging young, or teenage, stepsiblings, you can do this by making it clear that you're treating all the children within your home equally, while also leaning into the individual needs of each child.

Children acting up may not be bad behaviour. It could simply be their fear of being replaced or unloved by their biological parent. If you think it's tough for adults, it's super tough for children to adjust. They may also be worrying about fitting into the new family structure and feeling anxious about change.

It's hard to be honest about our insecurities, but the reality is that fear can also reveal itself in the dynamics between a new spouse and a former spouse. Concerns about loyalty, parenting styles, and influence over the children can create tension and conflict. Again, setting boundaries will help with this. Establish clear boundaries and roles in the co-parenting relationship to minimise misunderstandings. Try as much as possible to build mutual respect, focusing on the best interests of the children. This will not be a walk in the park. Where co-parenting is difficult, do your best to maintain a peaceful approach and pray. There is no heart that God cannot change.

 ## Stepping stones

- **Encourage activities that strengthen trust and unity** within your family. As much as possible, and where appropriate, ask everyone to participate in family decisions and respect one another's perspectives. Even if the final decision is down to the parents, children can still have a say in things like family trips, what's for dinner, and new purchases for the home.

- **You may want to consider family counselling** to address deep-rooted fears and to improve communication. This will be a brilliant investment in your family and will demonstrate to your children a sense of humility and acceptance that even we as adults don't have all the answers.

23

It's not working

'But blessed is the one who trusts in the Lord,
    whose confidence is in him.
They will be like a tree planted by the water
    that sends out its roots by the stream.
It does not fear when heat comes;
    its leaves are always green.
It has no worries in a year of drought
    and never fails to bear fruit.'
JEREMIAH 17:7–8

Our spouses may not always show up for us, and we need to prepare our hearts for that. This is the same in any marriage. They just may not always be emotionally available – we can't expect our loved ones to be on call for us emotionally all the time. They are not God.

When things are not working and conflicts and tension seem never-ending, it can feel awful. The question 'Where is God in all of this?' is a natural response, but he is with you, guiding you through the storm. Conversations without judgement will help. Find a way to agree that you will both use blame-free language. Create a safe space to do this when children are not present. Start with your relationship first, as where there is a stability between adults in a home, children feel safe and will naturally start to relax and settle. If there is division, they will exploit it and not even understand that this is what they are doing.

Ephesians 4:29 reminds us: 'Do not let any unwholesome talk come out of your mouths, but only what is helpful for building others up according to their needs, that it may benefit those who listen.'

Taking care of your own well-being is equally crucial in dealing with these challenges. Remember to set aside time for self-care and personal reflection. This could involve pursuing a hobby, engaging in physical exercise, or simply taking a break to recharge. By nurturing yourself, you are better equipped to handle the complexities of blending your family.

Be honest about your feelings and concerns; we are all human and no one is perfect. You must find a way to talk to each other. Sharing your experiences will lead to understanding, paving the way for a stronger, more resilient relationship. Actively listen to your partner's perspective, as well as acknowledging their feelings and working together to find common ground. Sometimes things will just feel unbearable. It's horrible when you feel like your continually being misunderstood, but the Bible says there is nothing too hard for God (Genesis 18:14).

Stepping stones

- **Practise patience and grace.** Remember that blending a family is a process that takes time. Think of it like this: it's not a quick microwave meal, but a Sunday roast – and the longer you take to marinate that meat, the better it will be. That microwave alternative will be a poor substitute. Take your time, and don't be hard on yourself. Things that are slow-cooked are better in the end. Be patient and extend grace even when it's difficult.

- **Explicitly agree with your partner that neither of you are perfect** and that you will not expect perfection from one another.

- **Seek God's wisdom and strength to navigate the challenges.** Philippians 4:6–7 offers this reassurance: 'Do not be anxious about anything, but in every situation, by prayer and petition, with thanksgiving, present your requests to God. And the peace of God, which transcends all understanding, will guard your hearts and minds in Christ Jesus.'

24

Discipline in darkness

'What I tell you in the dark, speak in the daylight; what is whispered in your ear, proclaim from the roofs.'
MATTHEW 10:27

God whispers his truths to us. Those moments of darkness, when everything seems to be going wrong, are not signs of his absence but opportunities for connection and revelation. Just as Jesus instructed his disciples, what we hear in these times of struggle should be proclaimed with courage and conviction.

For stepfamilies, the struggle is real. The merging of different backgrounds, traditions, and expectations can create crazy pressure. Yet, it is precisely in those moments of chaos and confusion that God desires to speak to us. He is not distant; he is present, ready to guide and comfort us. He is trying to teach you something special.

When panic sets in, be still and listen. There will be a message in the mess for you and your family. The message is not only meant to bring you peace but also to be shared with others. Jesus' words printed above are a command; it's not optional. Your experiences and the lessons you learn, in time, can become a beacon of hope and encouragement for other families navigating similar paths.

Embrace discipline in your darkest moments, and expect to hear from God. And when you do, let his words fill your heart and then boldly share them. Your story, shaped by God's whispers in the dark, has the power to illuminate the lives of others.

Stepping stones

- **Practise gratitude.** Find things to be thankful for. Gratitude shifts your focus from what's wrong to what's right, helping you see God's blessings.

- **Limit distractions.** There is a time to seek counsel and guidance from trusted friends. We also need to know when to retreat. Create a peaceful environment by reducing noise and distractions. This can help you stay focused on listening to God.

- **Journalling.** I've mentioned before that we should prepare for trials. Have a pen and paper handy, perhaps by your bed or in your car – wherever those places are that you know you can get quiet and alone with God. Write down your thoughts, prayers, and any revelations you receive. This can help you process your emotions and see God's hand in your life over time.

25

Jealousy

Love is patient, love is kind. It does not envy, it does not boast, it is not proud. It does not dishonour others, it is not self-seeking, it is not easily angered, it keeps no record of wrongs. Love does not delight in evil but rejoices with the truth. It always protects, always trusts, always hopes, always perseveres.

Love never fails. But where there are prophecies, they will cease; where there are tongues, they will be stilled; where there is knowledge, it will pass away.

1 CORINTHIANS 13:4–8

In stepfamilies, jealousy often surfaces as children and adults alike adjust to new roles and relationships. It's not uncommon for a child to feel threatened by a stepparent's presence or for a stepparent to feel insecure about their place in the family. Children may feel they must compete for the attention and affection of their parents. These feelings are natural, but they do not have to define your family dynamic.

I love the fact that 'Love never fails' is a sentence. Full stop. The love of God can handle jealousy, and by seeking God's wisdom you can embed peace and unity in your home. It may not happen overnight, and wisdom may involve just letting a lot of things go in the early years. There are some practical things you can do:

- Work together to create fair and inclusive family routines and ensure that everyone in your family feels heard.

- Understand that jealousy often stems from fear and insecurity. Reassure children of their unique and irreplaceable value.

- Creating new traditions can also help. Activities can range from family game nights, shared meals, or annual outings that everyone looks forward to. It's essential to cultivate an environment where everyone feels they belong and are part of the family narrative.

- If you're the stepparent, remember that adjusting to a new family structure takes time. Believe in yourself: you are the perfect person for this moment. Remember that everyone in your home will be navigating their path of change and fear.

- If you're the biological parent, reassure your spouse often that they're doing a great job.

- Draw strength from your faith and from each other. Reach out to trusted friends, family, or community leaders for support. Sometimes, an outside perspective can provide clarity and encouragement.

Stepping stones

- **Negative emotions are common and everyone experiences them** occasionally, even if the reasons are not always clear. Experiencing such feelings is a normal part of being human and does not reflect negatively on a person's character.

- **One practical thing we can all do when we are in the process of blending our families** is to manage our approach to social media. Everyone is not having a great time all the time. Every stepfamily will go through difficulties with experiencing jealousy and a range of other challenges.

- **Talk to your spouse and be honest.** The enemy wants to heap shame on us and make us feel bad, when the reality is that fear and insecurity when you are starting out on a new path is perfectly normal.

- **Pray this:** *Heavenly Father, we come before you seeking your guidance and strength as we navigate the complexities of our unique family. Help us to recognise and address the feelings of jealousy that may arise. Grant us the patience and understanding to develop relationships founded on your love. May our home be a place of peace and harmony, reflecting your grace and mercy. Amen.*

26

Our frailty is God's opportunity

But he said to me, 'My grace is sufficient for you, for my power is made perfect in weakness.' Therefore I will boast all the more gladly about my weaknesses, so that Christ's power may rest on me. That is why, for Christ's sake, I delight in weaknesses, in insults, in hardships, in persecutions, in difficulties. For when I am weak, then I am strong.
2 CORINTHIANS 12:9–11

Paul talks here about the method God used to keep him humble and to prevent him from boasting in his own abilities. God's strength and power are made perfect in our weakness. People who feel the need to be strong by themselves, who believe they are more superior and better than others and don't need help, are often living outside of the power of God. They increase in knowledge but prevent themselves from having a real understanding of what God desires to do through all of us. He wants to show us off so that he can be glorified. His words to us are: my grace is sufficient, lean on me, trust me, let me put my power on display in your life.

Don't try to be strong. When we relinquish our natural tendency to do our own thing, ask God for help and in humility acknowledge his greatness, his power will rest on us.

His strength is not made perfect in our strength – his strength is made perfect in our weakness. Pride must move aside, and humility needs to take centre stage. In stepfamilies this looks like laying aside pride when bonds feel fragile and comparisons arise. God's strength is not made perfect in us trying to hold it all together, but in our willingness to let him knit hearts his way.

You don't have to quote lots of scriptures or pray for an hour every day. There will be times in all our lives when roles and expectations will feel exhausting and when we will think, *I can't do this. I don't have the right skills/knowledge/background/temperament.* Be still. It is when we come to the end of ourselves, when we feel as though we have nothing left to give, that we will see God move in our circumstances. He is above all that we go through. That means he can take you and me in the midst of stepfamily dynamics and transform us into everything that he promised he would, if we will allow him to do so.

Stepping stones

- **Trust God and stop striving.** God has need of our weakness, and our strength is a hinderance that blocks us receiving the fullness of his power.

- **Our frailty is God's opportunity.** Our weakness is the position in which we can draw from his resources so that his glory may be seen. In the process of moving from blending to blended, this means letting go of the false security of believing that if we do things our own way it will work out for us; this is rarely the case with God.

- **God's way is not to take us out of the trial** but to give us the strength to handle it.

- **God's way is to see us die to pride** and not care about what others think during the process.

27

Happy home vs show home

I am not saying this because I am in need, for I have learned to be content whatever the circumstances.
PHILIPPIANS 4:11

In a perfect world, the best thing for a stepfamily to do is to move to a new home and start afresh. However, with established roots that isn't practical and it is unlikely to happen. I moved into my husband's home and found it hard for the first few years. Everything needed redoing. The house was a mess, and there were tears, pain, and moments of regret. I cried out to God endlessly, and I know he heard me, but during that season he was teaching me to respect the process, whereas initially I just wanted things my way.

It took ten years before we replaced our leather sofa (that I had inherited) with a brand new one. By the time we upgraded that old thing, I had become so attached to it I was trying to think about how we could keep it! 'By wisdom a house is built, and through understanding it is established' (Proverbs 24:3).

Don't give up because things are not going your way or life feels hard. Learn to be content in every season. Embrace the reality that there may be a good reason for God not to answer your prayer. As a couple, pursue God's purpose for your life, and ask him for the grace to live in contentment and peace. Stop looking at all the things that are not right or the material things you don't have. Stop feeling sorry for yourself; be a fountain and not a drain. Few people like people complaining around them all the time. Focus on what you do have.

We must learn to trust God completely if we are going to live peacefully. Material things are not important; your marriage and your mental health and well-being are.

Stepping stones

- **Be determined to be content.** Paul said I have learned to be content, so we see from his example that contentment is a process. We can develop and train ourselves to be in a consistent position of rest and joy.

- **Enjoy where you are right now on the way to where you're going.** Live life with a thankful heart. If your home is a mess or your stepchildren are acting out, thank God that you have a busy, loud house! And that you can hear and see the noise around you. You don't need a show home; you need a happy home. Children don't need perfection and lots of money to enjoy their lives, so just thank God for all the little things.

- **Pray this:** *Heavenly Father, help me to not complain, but to know that you are in complete control. Help us to work together as a team and be grateful for the blessing of family.*

Carl and Kate's story

Carl and Kate have been together for 17 years. Carl had two children prior to marrying Kate, who has no biological children. Carl's younger child came to live with them permanently when he was 11 years old.

Kate says:

> Both of our boys are great children. Carl's younger son initially wasn't accepting of me and saw me as a rival for his dad's affection. That surprised me as I automatically thought we would all get on!
>
> At times, the youngest child's behaviour could be quite challenging, often choosing to ignore me, and attempting to create an atmosphere of separation: the boys, my husband, and me on the outside. Looking back, I was very intentional about ensuring Carl had quality time with them. I never saw myself as their mother, simply a responsible adult, there to support my husband and his children. There was a conscious effort on my part not to want to impose.
>
> I remember feeling fine not attending school birthday parties as I knew the children wanted their parents there, and that was okay. Their peace and happiness are, and were always, the priority. However, even though I'd made these efforts, the youngest still rejected my presence, which was hard, and it was difficult not to take it personally. With time, that changed, and we all have a good relationship now. The boys are adults and have left home, but we all remain close.

Carl continues:

> Early on, I felt a little bit in the middle. I really wanted the boys to get on with my wife. For me, us being on the same page was

vital. Communication is key, as is honesty. I would say you need to spend time on your marriage; children can soak up a lot of your time and suddenly your marriage is on the backburner. There isn't a rule book for raising children, and I think accepting early on that things are not going to be perfect will help both the stepparent and bio-parent to manage expectations and take the pressure off one another.

As a father bringing children into the relationship, it was important for me to listen to my wife and for us to be caring and respectful of one another and not be dismissive of each other's feelings.

While raising children within a blended family environment can be hard, there is definitely hope.

Both Carl and Kate agree that the greatest joy of their stepparenting journey is to be proud of the children and to be seeing them now grown up as well-rounded adults.

Carl and Kate's top tips

- **Have boundaries.** Try not to spoil children with elaborate activities. Keep things the same and focus on the children's overall emotional well-being.

- **Things will not be perfect**; all you can do is your best. Don't take things personally. As children grow up and start to have their own relationships, they will start to see things very differently.

- **If you're the bio-parent bringing your children into the marriage**, listening and respecting your spouse's points of view is important for building a caring environment.

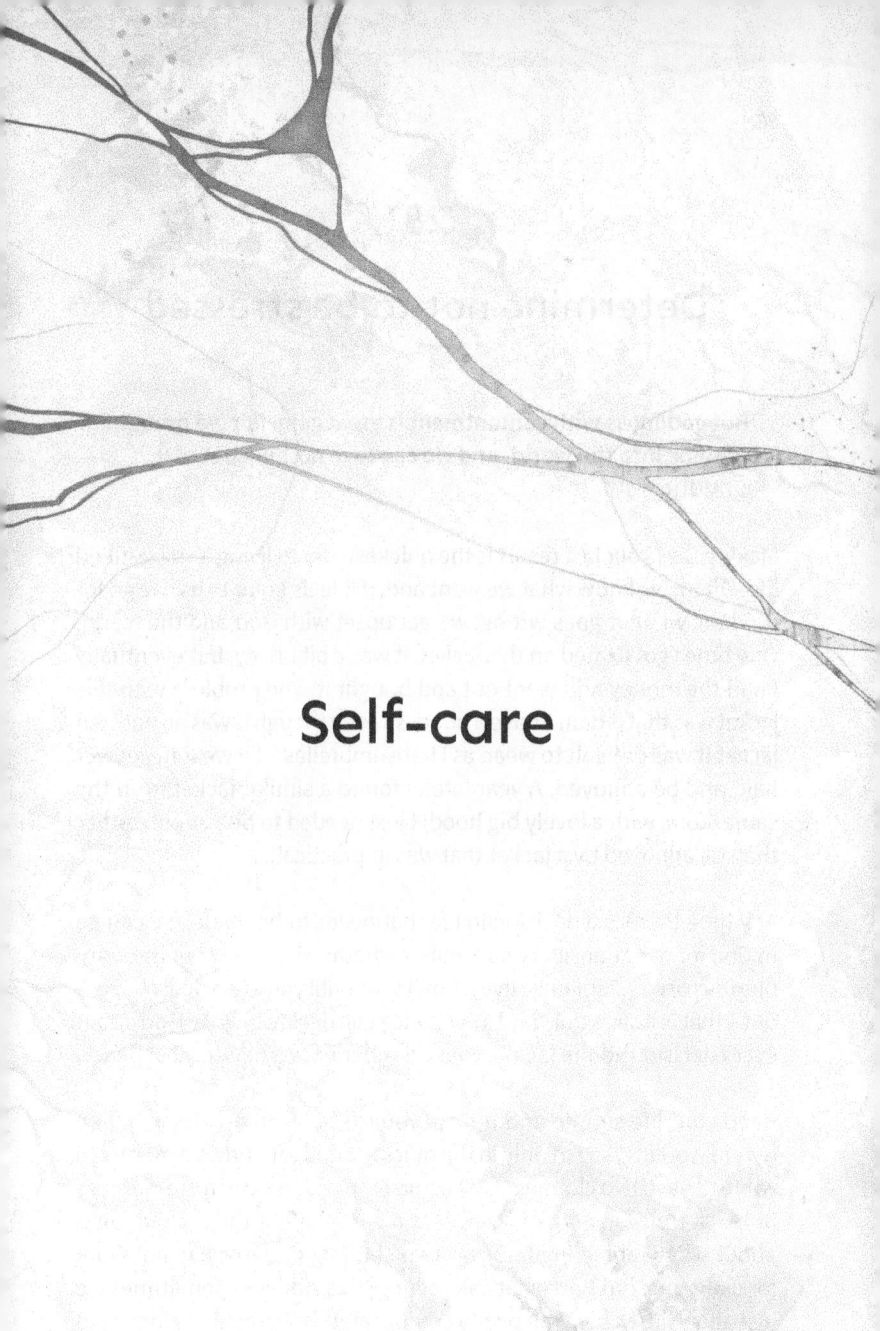

Self-care

28

Determine not to be stressed

**But godliness with contentment is great gain. For we brought
nothing into the world, and we can take nothing out of it.**
1 TIMOTHY 6:6–7

Making God your last resort is the quickest way to living a stress-filled
life. Often, we know what we want and, if it feels good to us, we go for
it. Then, when it goes wrong, we get upset with God and the world.
One time I got fixated on this jacket; it was a bit pricey, but eventually
I had the money and went out and bought it. The problem with this
jacket was that it didn't have a hood, so even though it was an autumn
jacket it was difficult to wear, as I hate umbrellas – I'd wear it, get wet
hair, and be annoyed. A year later, I found a similar jacket from the
same store, with a lovely big hood! I just needed to be patient, rather
than be annoyed by a jacket that was impractical.

Any time there is a decision in life that needs to be made, we can go
to God for direction; it doesn't matter whether it's a jacket or the complexities of our stepfamily lives. Don't wait until your idea doesn't work
out – that is a stressful way to live. Once you decide to go to God about
every decision you're facing, you will experience a new level of peace.

Keep your life simple and reduce your options. In my day job, I do
hybrid working, so I'm only in the office around four times a month. In
winter, I have two clothing choices: an orange dress and a blue jumper
or black trousers and a blazer. This means I'm not thinking for ages
about what I am going to wear. Two clothing options may not work
for everyone, but find what can reduce stress for you. Sometimes we
just allow life to become overly complicated with details, things, and
activities we don't need to be a part of. In stepfamilies, this can mean

learning to simplify our expectations, choosing peace over pressure, and trusting God to help us navigate roles and relationships without unnecessary strain.

Stepping stones

- **Think about the choices that you have to make** and then consider what gives you the most peace. If you can't decide, let peace make the call.

- **Timing is everything.** Sometimes we feel stressed because we're worried about a decision we need to make, but if you just waited a week or even 24 hours would it drastically change the outcome? The additional time to talk to a trusted friend to seek some good advice could quickly remove a potentially stressful outcome.

- **Reflect on these quotes:**

  Simplicity is the ultimate sophistication.
  Leonardo da Vinci

  Live simply so others may simply live.
  Mahatma Gandhi

  Life is really simple, but we insist on making it complicated.
  Confucius

29

Comparison the thief

Each one should test their own actions. Then they can take pride in themselves alone, without comparing themselves to someone else, for each one should carry their own load.
GALATIANS 6:4–5

It's easy to fall into the trap of comparison. We look at other families, blended or traditional, and wonder if we measure up. Are we doing enough? Are our relationships as strong? Are our children flourishing the way others seem to be? But comparison is a thief. It steals our joy, our peace, and our ability to fully embrace the unique assignment God has given us. Let's be honest; there will always be a family that is better off, people who are richer, smarter, children who present as perfect. But here's the thing: your family was God's idea. The way he equipped and designed each member of your household was his idea, and he doesn't make mistakes.

God never called us to live someone else's story. He has a specific plan for our families, one that is shaped by his wisdom and love. When we focus on what others are doing, we risk missing the beauty of what he is doing in our own homes. Success in God's eyes isn't about matching someone else's standard – it's about walking in obedience to his calling.

Instead of measuring our families against others, we should ask: Are we aligned with the assignment that God has for us? Are we seeking his guidance in our parenting, our relationships, and our daily interactions? Are we trusting him to shape our family according to his perfect will?

God's plan for your family is not a copy of someone else's – it is exclusively designed for you. You are only on this planet to be you. When we surrender comparison and embrace his purpose, we find peace and the confidence to walk boldly in alignment with the assignment he has given us.

Stepping stones

- **There is someone watching you, waiting for permission to be themselves** because you are embracing your uniqueness.

- **It is insulting to God to wish you had something that someone else has.** You are his masterpiece, the work of his hands; he fearfully and wonderfully made you and your beautiful family.

- **Even the things that we think are wrong with us, God has a purpose for.** The bottom line is that God knows what he's doing, so stop comparing!

- **Stop worrying about the things you don't have**, and embrace the freedom of not caring about what people think.

- **Love your life and your lane.** Celebrate yourself and your family, and celebrate others!

30

Cast your cares

Cast all of your anxiety on him because he cares for you.
1 PETER 5:7

I moved from a one-bedroom flat into my husband's three-bedroom house after our wedding. Previously, he had shared the house with his children and ex-wife. I felt uncomfortable in the house, because nothing felt like me, and I constantly felt like a tenant. My new home had this looming air of brokenness in every room. The walls were familiar with the language of divorce.

I wanted to move and start afresh. I made my dissatisfaction clear – not necessarily in a loud and shouty way, but I quietly made my discontentment felt on a regular basis. I couldn't see the huge blessing in the mess that God had given me. He had literally laid a table for us in the midst of our enemies, but initially I couldn't see it.

There is nothing positive about worry and anxiety. These are emotions that will not help you – in fact, stress can kill you. Stop worrying; it's a manifestation of pride. That's hard for me even to write, as I have done my fair share of worrying. But we are created by God to be dependent on him. We are not designed to handle our problems ourselves.

If you're living in a home right now that you didn't choose, perhaps change your view to see that the environment chose you. Take your time to think about all the things that God has done for you, and be patient, as your change will come.

Stepping stones

- **Stop trying to do things** in your own strength.

- **Whatever you allow to preoccupy your mind** will reveal itself in your behaviour. Train yourself to bring every thought captive to the obedience of biblical principles.

- **Stop worrying thoughts in their tracks before they start.** When you first start doing this, you will feel like there is always a negative or worrying thought every second – but keep at it. The more you continue to replace worry with a positive thought or scripture, your heart will become fuller with God's word and those worrying tendencies will become smaller and smaller.

31

Pursue peace

**You will keep in perfect peace
  those whose minds are steadfast,
  because they trust in you.**
ISAIAH 26:3

In the busyness of daily life and challenging times, finding peace can seem elusive. In stepfamilies, where relationships and routines can feel complicated, that peace can feel particularly hard to grasp. Yet the Bible promises us a peace that transcends all understanding, that's perfect, and that's unwavering to all.

I love the Bible; it shows us again and again that God does detail. The peace promised in Isaiah 26:3 isn't just any kind of peace; it's perfect peace!

It's a calm that is not dependent on our circumstances. Everyone who chooses to focus on God and trust him, no matter what, is promised perfect peace that defies human understanding. And it can impact every aspect of our lives. When we are connected to God, he promises us an eventual good outcome. Romans 8:28 reminds us: 'And we know that in all things God works for the good of those who love him, who have been called according to his purpose.'

Jesus is our ultimate example. In Mark 4:39, we see him waking up from his sleep and calming a literal storm with his words, 'Peace! Be still!' (ESV). The Bible says the storm was ferocious with violent winds. While the disciples were stressing, Jesus was sleeping. Just as he brought peace to the winds and waves, he can bring peace to our personal storms. His peace can move you from chaos to calm and bring harmony to hearts that are learning to grow together.

Our Christian faith compels us to not conform to the world's way of doing things. This means not relying on circumstances and material things to provide us with a temporary form of 'unperfect' peace. Rather, spending time in God's word helps us shift our focus from our problems to his promises.

Prayer is our lifeline to God. When we present our worries and concerns to him, we experience a divine exchange: our anxieties for his peace. Take time each day to pray specifically for peace in your family.

Remember, God's peace is not the absence of trouble and it doesn't always come with comfort; rather it is the promise of the presence of God in the midst of it all. Trust in him and experience his perfect peace, even in the most turbulent times.

 **Stepping stones**

- **Create a peaceful and nurturing environment in your home.** This could mean setting aside a quiet space for prayer, using calming music, or engaging in activities that promote peace within your family. This is especially meaningful in blended households, where creating a sense of unity and calm can help everyone to feel secure and loved.

- **Self-care is a crucial part of our spiritual well-being.** Going for walks daily, watching your favourite type of movie, and spending time with friends are all godly ways to protect the peace of God in your life.

- **Take mindfulness breaks throughout your day** to breathe and focus your thoughts on God's promises.

- **Physical activity** can significantly boost your mood and mental clarity.

- **Ensure you're getting enough sleep**. It will be difficult to maintain a calm and focused mind if you're tired.

- **Ask God for the grace to trust** and keep your mind steadfastly focused on him.

- **Identify at least three of these points** that you will incorporate into your daily routine today.

32

Just relax

> 'Peace I leave with you; my peace I give you. I do not give to
> you as the world gives. Do not let your hearts be troubled and
> do not be afraid.'
> JOHN 14:27

In the first few years of my marriage, I remember always asking my
stepson to do something and then five minutes later I'd overhear my
stepdaughter telling him to do the exact opposite – or the same thing a
different way. My husband would consistently turn a blind eye. Initially
it used to infuriate me. I felt unsupported, like an outsider in my own
home. But how could I possibly go up against a seven-year-old girl?
Even when I asked her kindly not to ignore my request, she didn't listen.

It took me a good while to understand that she wasn't being disobe-
dient. She was simply and understandably in survival mode, looking
after her younger brother and herself the only way she knew how. She
didn't choose to be ferried around from one house to the next every
other weekend; she was handling her hustle the only way her little
emotions could.

Let things go; everything doesn't have to be perfect. If everyone is 'kind
of' happy in the early stages, that's okay. We will never enjoy the gift
of peace without being willing to accept, adjust, and adapt.

Acceptance involves embracing the new family structure and the
individuals within it, with all their quirks and histories. It helps in
creating an environment where everyone feels valued and understood.
It's about acknowledging that family members might have different
ways of doing things and respecting those differences. Acceptance is

essential for embedding a sense of belonging and stability, especially for children who might be adjusting to a new world order. Not taking everything too seriously will eventually develop a team spirit where everyone feels included and all members of your family can thrive.

Stepping stones

- **Learn to rest.** Don't overthink everything.

- **Finding rest for the soul helps reduce stress and anxiety.** When everyone in your home is at peace, you are more capable of embedding a harmonious and loving environment.

- **Rest isn't just about physical rest**; it's also a deep spiritual calm that can come from letting go and letting God.

- **Enjoy the journey.**

- **Say out loud:** *I am determined to enjoy my life, every area of my life: my marriage, my children, my job. I'm grateful for what God has done for me. I'm proud of myself. I love the family that God has given me. I might not be where I want to be, but I'm on my way to great things and I'm excited.*

33

Self-care

'Come to me, all you who are weary and burdened, and I will give you rest. Take my yoke upon you and learn from me, for I am gentle and humble in heart, and you will find rest for your souls. For my yoke is easy and my burden is light.'
MATTHEW 11:28–30

When was the last time you took a day or even a weekend out for yourself? At the start of any flight, the crew takes you through safety and emergency procedures, emphasising the importance of putting on your life jacket before helping others. Essentially: when you help yourself first, you're then in a better position to help someone else.

'Me time' is essential and you deserve it. A well-rested mind is a more patient and loving one. Adults should work together so that both of you allow each other to do the things that will help you relax. Make this an essential part of your plan at the start of each year. 'Me time' should be once a week, even if it's just a couple of hours. Additionally, aim to have a night away by yourself once a year, and as a couple, plan a weekend away without your children.

None of this is a nice-to-do; it's crucial. Individually, my husband and I will both have time away by ourselves; even if these are work trips, it is still a change of scenery and time by yourself to think. We will then have a weekend alone together once a year.

Self-care is not selfish; it is vital for maintaining your emotional, mental, and physical well-being. Our families come with unique challenges and stressors that can easily lead to burnout if not managed properly. Taking time for yourself allows you to recharge, reflect, and return to those you love with a renewed sense of purpose and energy. You are also modelling how to do relationships well and demonstrating to your children the importance of looking after yourself.

Stepping stones

- **Remember, it's okay to ask for help** and lean on your support system. Your partner, friends, and family can offer valuable assistance and understanding. Asking for help is honourable.

- **Whether it's reading a book, going for a walk,** practising a hobby, or simply enjoying a quiet moment with a cup of tea, these small acts of self-care can make a significant difference in your overall well-being.

- **By taking time for you, you are the best version of yourself** for your family. Embrace the practice of self-care, and you will find that it not only benefits you but also strengthens your relationships and your ability to nurture and support your loved ones.

34

Laughter works

A cheerful heart is like good medicine,
but a crushed spirit dries up the bones.
PROVERBS 17:22

Laughter is a gift from God. It can help manage stress, fear, and worry, and it can stimulate healing. Any doctor will tell you that it provides strong medical, psychological, and social benefits.

Look for opportunities to laugh in your relationship and try to not take things too seriously. This is easier said than done, when you're constantly going between confusion and exasperation and walking that tightrope of hurt feelings. We might not think we can laugh under pressure, but we can, and we must if we are going to make it through. Jesus said, 'In the world you will have tribulation; but be of good cheer, I have overcome the world' (John 16:33, NKJV).

At the back of our house, we can sometimes get the odd mouse sneak into our laundry area in winter. The funny thing is that they tend to appear when I have had an argument with my husband. I'll go to bed cross, then get up in the morning, go downstairs, and I'll peer through the glass door, and there will be that small furry tenant! The only way to evict that tenant? My husband, along with speedily remembering all the scriptures in the Bible about forgiveness. I guess if God can use a donkey (Numbers 22—24), he can use mice too!

Let's not allow the enemy to steal our joy to the point where we don't see the funny side of things. You can't laugh and be angry, and you can't laugh and worry. If you allow it to, laughter can lead you into a more positive perspective. Joy, peace, and purpose can come out of pain. Trust that things can change and enjoy the adventure.

Stepping stones

- **Put time in your schedule for things that you know will bring you joy.** Remember that laughter helps to boost your immune system.

- **Nothing works faster** or more dependably to bring your mind and body back into balance than a good laugh.

- **Laughing frequently** is a great way to overcome problems, while also enhancing your relationships and supporting both physical and emotional health. Best of all, this priceless medicine is fun and free.

- **Often in marriage we are so focused on transactional activities**, like the school run, who's taking the kids to their clubs, or navigating difficult conversations with an ex-partner. Make a commitment to do something once a week that is fun.

Jason's story

**And we know that in all things God works for the good of those
who love him, who have been called according to his purpose.**
ROMANS 8:28

Being 17 isn't easy. It's that weird space between childhood and adulthood where you're expected to figure things out but still feel lost. Add
a stepmother and a second family into the mix, and life can feel even
more complicated.

I won't lie – when my dad remarried, I wasn't happy. It felt like my world
was shifting, like I had to make room for people I didn't ask for. I missed
the way things used to be, and I wondered if loving my stepmother or
new brother and sister meant I was betraying my mum.

But God doesn't make mistakes. He places people in our lives for a reason, even when it's hard to see at first. Instead of fighting the changes,
I started asking him to help me understand. And slowly, he did.

I realised my stepmother wasn't trying to replace my mum – she was
just trying to love me in the way she knew how. My father had further
children with my stepmum, and I now had two siblings who were much
younger than me. Over time, I realised that they weren't competition –
they were just as confused as I was, trying to navigate our new and
complex family dynamic. And my dad? He was still my dad, even if life
looked different now.

One night, after another awkward dinner followed by an argument,
I read Romans 8:28. I'd heard it before, but this time, it hit differently:
'In all things God works for the good.' Even in blended families. Even
in change. Even when I didn't like it.

I won't pretend everything is perfect now. There are still tough days, moments when I feel like an outsider or when old wounds resurface. But I'm learning that family isn't about having the perfect setup – it's about love, grace, and letting God work through the mess.

So, if you're struggling with a stepparent or a second family, know this: God is still writing your story. He hasn't forgotten you. And maybe – just maybe – he's building something even better than you imagined.

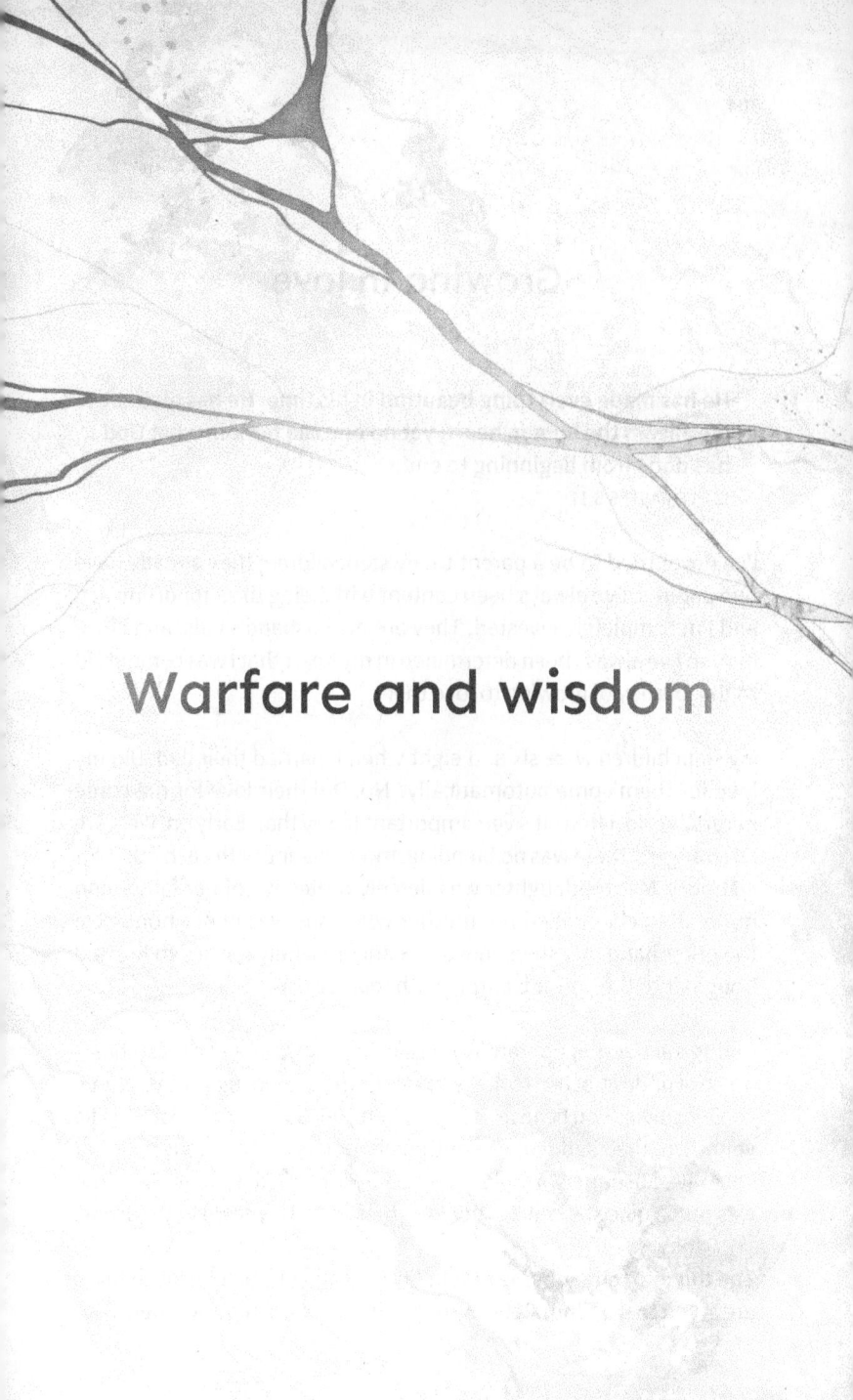

Warfare and wisdom

35

Growing in love

He has made everything beautiful in his time. He has also set eternity in the human heart; yet no one can fathom what God has done from beginning to end.
ECCLESIASTES 3:11

I've never tried to be a parent to my stepchildren; they already have two parents. I've always been content with being the supporting act, and I'm completely invested. They are my husband's kids, and I love him, so I've always been determined in my heart that I was committed to the journey of growing to love them.

My stepchildren were six and eight when I married their dad. Did my love for them come automatically? No. Did their love for me come naturally? No. I think it's very important to say that. Early on, we were all strangers; there was no blending, more bearing with each other for 48 hours. My stepdaughter was fiercely protective of her father and quite often channelled her mother when she was in our home. On the other hand, my stepson was six and generally just loved life and bought into the new adventure with relative ease.

Biological parents operate from a position of DNA – that also has a sense of pride attached to it. Stepparenting is psychologically a lot more challenging as you have moments when your stepkids almost feel like your own, then suddenly something happens that reminds you that you have absolutely no say in a complex logistical arrangement that was put in place by court order long before you came on to the scene.

The thing to remember is that in Christ, even our biological children are gifted to us. Ultimately, we only have stewardship over them. Our role is simply to lovingly guide and prepare them for adulthood. You can do that with your stepchildren too and your love for them will develop over time. Don't force it; be patient. God makes everything beautiful in his time.

Stepping stones

- **Please don't be hard on yourself.** If you're the stepparent, don't worry if you don't feel a pure love for your stepchildren straight away – just be committed to the journey.

- **If you're the biological parent, give your spouse time, space, and grace** to develop into their new role. Don't force them into bonding scenarios with your children if they are telling you that's not something they are comfortable with.

- **Biological parents: your spouse may forget** which days the children are coming over and get confused with all the extracurricular activities. That's okay. Working together as a team you will get there.

- **If your union has followed the bereavement of a parent**, your new partner will try their best to remember key anniversaries and moments that may lead to reflection and sadness among family members. But in the busyness of life they may forget. Again, if we all assume positive intent and that everyone is trying their best, it will help.

- **Put your marriage first always.** In a traditional setup, the marriage always comes first, and a couple have time together to learn about each other prior to children coming into the equation. In a stepfamily home, it's so much more complex as you try to establish your marriage but also factor in the vital needs of children who didn't ask for such seismic change! If you demonstrate an unswerving love for one another, that will translate into stability into your home. Children thrive when there is stability.

36

Feeling like an outsider?

Do not be anxious about anything, but in every situation, by prayer and petition, with thanksgiving, present your requests to God. And the peace of God, which transcends all understanding, will guard your hearts and your minds in Christ Jesus
PHILIPPIANS 4:6-7

Not all experiences are positive between stepparents and stepchildren; however, many stepparents have developed healthy lifelong relationships with their stepchildren. I'm grateful that I am one of them, and my prayer is that you can be too. Be wise; relationships take time. Focus on being a caring and responsible adult, as opposed to trying to win your stepchildren over. Trying to compete for your stepchildren's affection with their bio-parent is never going to work. Get used to understanding that there will always be an inner circle that you will not be privy to and that's okay.

When feelings of insecurity arise, because you find yourself on the periphery and key conversations are happening between the bio-parent without you, take a moment to pray. Prayer works. Remember your spouse loves you, chose you, and entrusted you with their most precious gift: their children. While it's natural to feel overshadowed or even threatened by history and memories you weren't part of, shift your focus to the new memories you are building together.

As a stepparent, your presence represents a new chapter, one filled with the promise of hope and joy.

Children will play up, even older children. A changed family dynamic can be very unsettling for them, and they may not know how to behave.

They may really like you and feel a sense of guilt that they're betraying their bio-parent by getting closer to you. They may dislike you and not know why. Be patient. The longer you're on the stepparent journey, the more you start to realise that sacrificial giving and selflessness will be the key to your success. Let go of anxiety – you've got this!

Stepping stones

- **Through prayer, guard your heart** from those voices in your head telling you that you are not enough.

- **Children don't always know how to effectively express themselves.** They are dealing with loss and change in the best way they can. Sometimes that may bring chaos to your world and sometimes it may be an opportunity for you to connect with them. Ask God to help you to discern the moment and, if in doubt, always be led by them.

- **Greater is he that is in you** (1 John 4:4) and you can do all things through Christ who strengthens you (Philippians 4:13). You have the capacity to be calm and rational and to consistently take the position of emotional maturity when you are with your spouse and their children. If you feel the need to let off some steam, there is always your prayer space or a trusted friend. Do everything you can to not lose your cool with your stepchildren.

37

Biological vs stepchildren

Start children off on the way they should go,
and even when they are old they will not turn from it.
PROVERBS 22:6

It's easy to pour all your energy into trying to win over stepchildren,
hoping to bridge gaps and solidify relationships. However, as you work
to cultivate love and connection within your spouse's children, your
biological children still need you.

God has entrusted your biological children to you from birth. They look
to you for guidance, stability, and love – not just when circumstances
allow, but continuously. Your first ministry as a parent is to the children
whom God has given you to raise. While stepchildren are a precious
part of your family, they ultimately have another biological parent
responsible for their primary upbringing.

Putting plans on pause – delaying holidays, holding off celebrations,
or avoiding outings – can unintentionally make biological children feel
second place in their own home. Their childhood is happening now.
They deserve to create memories, have fun, and experience a full life.

Stepparenting is about grace, patience, and wisdom. Investing in stepchildren is a noble effort, but not at the expense of neglecting those
who solely depend on you. If you deplete yourself entirely, attempting
to fix relationships beyond your control, your biological children may
end up feeling overlooked and resent you for it. They deserve consistency, joy, and your undivided love and attention.

How to balance the journey with biblical wisdom:

- **Prioritise your household.** 1 Timothy 5:8 reminds us that we are called to provide for our families. If you are emotionally drained trying to connect with a resistant stepchild, step back and refocus on maintaining peace and stability for your biological children.

- God calls us to **steward every child we raise with wisdom**. Your biological children need to experience joy today – not just when schedules align. Love generously, embrace flexibility, and trust that God will strengthen your family as you walk in wisdom and grace.

- **Rest in God's sovereignty.** You are not called to be everything for everyone. Surrender the things you cannot change, and trust that God's plan will unfold in time.

Stepping stones

- **Focus on unity, not control.** You can't always change attitudes, but you can create an atmosphere of love and peace.

- **Your biological children's lives continue** regardless of stepchildren's schedules. If your stepchildren are not with you every day, it doesn't mean your biological children must be in waiting mode.

- **Accept what you cannot change.** Some wounds run deep, and healing takes time. Offer love, but don't force what isn't ready.

- **Your children come first.** Do not get to the place of exhaustion and stress over children that are ultimately not yours. Don't lose yourself in the stepparenting role and lose sight of your own children's emotional needs. You don't have to feel guilty about putting them first. They should be protected from the emotional crossfire of stepfamily life.

- **Healthy family dynamics should not be dictated** by external custody arrangements.

38

The battle belongs to the Lord

He said: 'Listen, King Jehoshaphat and all who live in Judah and Jerusalem! This is what the Lord says to you: "Do not be afraid or discouraged because of this vast army. For the battle is not yours, but God's."'
2 CHRONICLES 20:15

You will never win if you're fighting battles on your own. God has never lost a battle; he always has a plan and if we follow it, we will win. Praise stills the enemy. If we praise God during our battles, we send confusion to the camp of the enemy, and if we worship God for his attributes over time, we will start to see his nature flow out from our lives. There is a divine exchange that is automatic when we hide ourselves under the shadow of the Almighty and watch him work.

Fill your home with praise and worship; I know this may not work for everyone, but I take a hard line about the music I allow in our environment. All my children know they will never hear secular music being blared from the speakers in our home. Why? Because it doesn't set the right atmosphere. The rules may bend slightly in the car, but I keep a tight rein on it!

When worship is the anthem of your heart and praise is your battle cry, that sound will flood out and touch the lives of those around you.

We all have moments when we question God, and that is okay. When it comes to what is taking place in your home, find one Bible verse and stand on it. For example, this is one I like to hold on to: 'He who began a good work in you will carry it on to completion' (Philippians 1:6).

Speak the word of faith over your family even when your happy ending isn't visible.

The enemy's strategy is always to use our small worldview against us. He wants us to think that what we physically see in our moment of difficulty is all there is. The beautiful worship song 'Be Magnified' by Lynn DeShazo illustrates this. It talks about the moments when we make God too small in our eyes and instead believe the lies the enemy presents us with.

Stepping stone

- **Look for 'Be Magnified' and add it to your worship playlist.** Remember, there is a spiritual realm where God and the hosts of heaven are fighting for us to win. If we allow our viewpoint to focus on what is in front of us, only fear will win.

39

Put on the whole armour of God

Finally, be strong in the Lord and in his mighty power. Put on the full armour of God, so that you can take your stand against the devil's schemes. For our struggle is not against flesh and blood, but against the rulers, against the authorities, against the powers of this dark world and against the spiritual forces of evil in the heavenly realms. Therefore put on the full armour of God, so that when the day of evil comes, you may be able to stand your ground, and after you have done everything, to stand.
EPHESIANS 6:10–13

Marriage is a covenant that mirrors the relationship between Christ and the church. It is a divine representation of unity, love, and commitment. A Christ-centred marriage stands as a powerful testimony to God's love and faithfulness towards us.

This makes the call to protect and nurture our families so very important. The enemy targets marriages because he knows that a strong, united family is a fortress of faith and love. The Bible says that the thief comes to steal, kill, and destroy (John 10:10). Thieves are looking for things that are valuable. They don't waste time breaking into empty houses.

If we remember that stepfamilies are most often borne out of brokenness, you start to understand that the devil thought he had won. However, redemption, restoration, and healing have stepped in and thwarted his plan. Stepfamilies are Easter people! The resurrection power of Jesus is embodied in our homes. The enemy is not content to roll over and play dead.

If the enemy is regularly trying to play havoc in your home, it means the dreams you have for your family are highly valuable and the devil wants to steal them and leave you hopeless. He can see the potential you have to do great things.

To withstand these attacks, we must all put on the full armour of God daily through prayer. How can we do this?

- **Belt of truth.** Commit to transparency in your marriage. For example, if you get a speeding fine, don't hide it from your spouse! You'll be amazed how small foxes like this turn into raging fires that challenge the peace in our homes.

- **Breastplate of righteousness.** Have integrity in everything you do; be right standing always, even in the face of losing out as a result.

- **Feet shod with the gospel of peace.** Share your faith with others, individually and together. Try your best to be a peaceful person. Look for solutions.

- **Shield of faith.** Trust in God's promises completely and use your faith to distinguish the enemy's fiery arrows. An example of a fiery arrow might be random arguments that come out of nowhere. Nip them in the bud quickly and serve notice to energy-sapping petty quarrels.

- **Helmet of salvation.** Protect your mind from negative thoughts. When thoughts of doubt and despair enter your mind, immediately focus on hope. The more you exercise your thought life in this area, the easier it will become.

- **Sword of the Spirit.** Read your Bible daily. Have a plan that works for you, as long as you are meditating on at least one scripture for the day, that's a good place to start. This will help keep your mind healthy and focused on the right things.

Stepping stones

- **We will never outgrow warfare.** You will have to get comfortable with being a fighter, when you have a God-honouring marriage. In God, we are winners, and the devil doesn't want us to win.

- **Remember that God never loses a battle.** He has a plan, and if we follow it, we win.

- **Don't add fuel to the fire.** A fire needs heat, fuel, and oxygen to burn brightly. Don't endlessly talk about your trial, especially with the wrong people, as this is both fuel and oxygen that is sustaining the problem and making it worse. Follow God's battle plan – keep your eyes on him and your conversation full of his word. He will put the fire out.

40

Give God control

'Look at the birds of the air; they do not sow or reap or store away in barns, and yet your heavenly Father feeds them. Are you not much more valuable than they? Can any one of you by worrying add a single hour to your life?

'And why do you worry about clothes? See how the flowers of the field grow. They do not labour or spin. Yet I tell you that not even Solomon in all his splendour was dressed like one of these. If that is how God clothes the grass of the field, which is here today and tomorrow is thrown into the fire, will he not much more clothe you – you of little faith? So do not worry, saying, "What shall we eat?" or "What shall we drink?" or "What shall we wear?" For the pagans run after all these things, and your heavenly Father knows that you need them. But seek first his kingdom and his righteousness, and all these things will be given to you as well. Therefore do not worry about tomorrow, for tomorrow will worry about itself. Each day has enough trouble of its own.'

MATTHEW 6:26–34

A stepparent can be in the middle, on the outside, or in the background. Sometimes we are the main character, sometimes the supporting act, and sometimes we're the stagehand. We will suffer burnout if we try to juggle and control all these different dynamics on our own. Don't try to control and be the main character when, at that time, it's best to be the supporting act. I know it's hard – I'm not going to say I don't like to be the centre of attention at times!

Control is an illusion; it never works. God's way may be hard, but it's always the best option. He will take the burden from you, and in exchange give you rest for your soul. In exchange for worry and anxiety, you can receive peace and power. If you are finding it hard giving God full control through prayer alone, grab a piece of paper and write down the areas of your life that you need to surrender. Surrendering is a lifelong process, intended to keep us dependent on God.

We must be intentional about letting go. I remember in the early days of our marriage I used to make lots of notes and keep a record of the difficulties we were having with my husband's ex-wife. I'd screen-grab text messages and save them, just in case something went really wrong, and we needed proof of behaviour that wasn't right. We all have a human tendency to self-protect. I felt it was my job to control the outcome as I didn't have the emotional connection with the children that my husband had. Then one day, I just stopped. What was I trying to prove? I couldn't protect him; only God could.

Pain can move us forward in our spiritual journeys just as much as success, so we must trust God and trust the process.

 ## Stepping stones

- **Keep a journal** about the things you're worried about and pray about them every day until you see change in those areas.

- **Look after your mental health and well-being.** Switch off and go for walks outside and see his beauty and splendour in nature. You will quickly start to see the reality that, if God can look after the trees of the field and the birds of the air, it's straightforward for him to take care of you and yours. We call stepfamilies complex, when in fact they may be so for us, but nothing is too hard for our God.

41

Respect

Be completely humble and gentle; be patient, bearing with one another in love.
EPHESIANS 4:2

Sometimes we just don't have the bandwidth to be nice. We are tired, and our flesh wants to make its point and be heard – or maybe that's just me! However, healthy relationships are founded on mutual respect; it is vital if you want to have a peaceful home.

Sometimes the reasons for respect are obvious, and at other times we find it difficult to understand why we must ask our spouse before making big decisions, as well as involving children. There will be times when we don't like doing certain things, but we can learn to develop an enjoyment and love for them if it means we are making our spouse and children happy.

Respect is fragile. It can take years to build and can be broken in a second and become difficult to restore. That's why we must always have it at the front of our minds as a key asset in our toolbox for a healthy home.

Respecting your spouse means loving them unconditionally and allowing them the space to be themselves. It means never putting them in the position where they are forced to be someone they're not.

It means helping one another to see that you genuinely acknowledge each other's thoughts, ideas, and feelings – and that you're willing to be guided by them, even if you don't fully understand. Work together as a team to find common ground. Be honest and make clear that protecting each other's emotions is a priority even if you get it wrong sometimes – we all do. Don't try to change your spouse; only God can do that.

This isn't just about adults; it cascades down to your children as well. Find ways to bring them into decision-making and help them to understand that their opinions and ideas count. This will help everyone to have a sense of ownership of the vision for your family.

Stepping stones

- Remember that **respect increases trust and leads to better communication.** It's a must-have, not a nice-to-have. It's like the bread, milk, and butter on the shopping list. If you forget these items, you have to return to the shop. If you forget about respect, you have to circle back and pick it up!

- In a family where **everyone is being treated with respect**, the mental health and well-being of everyone will be protected.

- Respect also extends to former spouses and those who are outside your family unit but have influence. **Pray for the fruit of the Spirit to be developed in your lives** (see Galatians 5:22–23), as walking in them will make it much easier to be nice at times when it may be difficult.

Priscilla's story

Priscilla has been married for nine years and has founded a club for stepmums. Together, her and her husband have six children, three of whom they had together. Priscilla has two stepchildren and had a child prior to meeting her husband. Her stepchildren would rarely acknowledge her initially and her approach was to carry on as best as she could, so the atmosphere didn't impact on her biological children.

Priscilla says:

> The pressure of feeling alone is immense and you spend a lot of time feeling stuck. There were constant tensions between former partners and a husband who was passive. I just didn't feel supported. It was really hard trying to get to grips with all the different personalities in the house. It was difficult, as I hadn't grown up in a house with conflict. Church is great; however, the understanding of my unique family set up just isn't catered for, so you are always feeling othered.

Looking back, she could see how things could have been managed differently. She used avoidance and didn't speak to her friends about what she was going through. They couldn't possibly relate to her experience. Today she is in a better place, setting up the stepmum's club was a way to support other people and take the focus off herself.

> I'd advise anyone about to form a stepfamily to embrace the reality that initially it will not be easy, but that things will get better. Pieces from different jigsaw puzzles don't fit together. Be aware that it will be hard. At the same time, remember that a Picasso painting can have many interpretations; you can make it your kind of perfect. No one outside of your family can tell you what

you see in the painting that is your family. You decide ultimately what you want it to be.

Priscilla strongly believes that, as Christ died for us all, the church could do a lot more to support families that are not traditional and address divorce in a more restorative way as it happens.

Today, she is proud that she can say that she has been blessed to be able to speak into her stepchildren's life. Her approach is more balanced, and she considers it an honour to pray for them. As her firstborn child was a girl, her daughter now has two big brothers who can look after her – something she never had personally growing up and always wanted; however, God had planned and purposed it that way for her little girl.

Priscilla's top tips

- **Pray and know God is in control.** My favourite verse of scripture is Romans 8:18: 'I consider that our present sufferings are not worth comparing with the glory that will be revealed in us.'

- **God has a plan for us and it's important to hold on to that.** Every marriage has its challenges and things will improve with time. Know that God is working it all out for your good and that he will ultimately be glorified in your union.

- **Try to not be too hard on each other, and talk.** Don't allow the challenges with difficult ex-spouses to spill over into your relationship. Don't be passive; find a way to talk and seek out the right people to counsel you if you're really struggling.

Mercy and forgiveness

42

Forgiving one another

Get rid of all bitterness, rage and anger, brawling and slander, along with every form of malice. Be kind and compassionate to one another, forgiving each other, just as in Christ God forgave you.
EPHESIANS 4:31–32

We know as Christians that we are commanded to forgive, but it can be deeply difficult to do so when we believe we've been wronged. The stepfamily is especially vulnerable to misunderstanding, and conflict can regularly arise from past hurts. Grief can take its time to heal, and a spouse may suddenly experience triggers related to the loss of a loved one and not know how to express themselves. This may present in poor behaviour. Forgiveness always lies at the heart of any strong relationship. Good marriages are often just two people whose imperfections are compatible, where each person decides to forgive, believe the best, and move forward in love.

When we demonstrate forgiveness in our marriage, we set a positive example for our children. It is vital for everyone's overall well-being, including former spouses who are not within our home environment. Children, who can often feel incredibly vulnerable when learning to navigate a new routine, really need our compassion. Forgiveness becomes vital when they act out as they process the trauma of bereavement or divorce. Forgiveness will help to nurture a supportive and safe family unit for everyone involved.

But how do we forgive when it feels hard? Remember the price Jesus paid on the cross, forgiving us of all our sins? We are not excusing or minimising wrongdoing; rather, we are called to imitate Christ's sacrifice by extending grace and mercy to others, no matter what the offence. We will also release ourselves from the bondage of resentment.

Practically, we must consider the stress and toll unforgiveness will ultimately take on our bodies. Studies have found that the act of forgiveness can reap significant benefits on our health, lowering the risk of a heart attack, high blood pressure and depression, and improving our cholesterol levels and sleep. So, if you're really struggling in this area, let that person go for you!

Stepping stones

- **If you're really struggling with unforgiveness** in your marriage, please get counselling. Or speak to trusted friends who can help you.

- **Remember, in forgiving we are not ignoring or condoning**; rather, we are imitating Christ and putting our trust in his grace being sufficient to bring healing and restoration.

- **While divorced couples may be glad to see the back of one another**, in many ways divorce can seem like a death to children. It is almost certainly the death of a family unit that once was. Forgiving their early behaviour is key to supporting them into a new and healthy emotional space. Do not hold grudges against children of any age.

- **Husbands and wives who model forgiveness** send a strong message to their children; you are teaching them how to handle conflict in a healthy way.

- **Do not to keep a record of wrongs**; love doesn't do this, and it will not lead to peace. Your spouse will find it deeply hurtful if every time there is a conflict, you bring up something that happened a year ago.

43

Forgiving yourself

Therefore, there is now no condemnation for those who are in Christ Jesus, because through Christ Jesus the law of the Spirit who gives life has set you free from the law of sin and death.
ROMANS 8:1–2

Through faith in Christ, we are free of condemnation and can embrace grace and forgiveness. This is especially meaningful in the context of a stepfamily, where feelings of guilt and inadequacy may arise.

Modelling self-forgiveness is vital for personal growth. We all make mistakes, but failure gives us a beautiful gift: experience. You must forgive yourself, as holding on to regret will negatively impact your emotional well-being. Conversely, forgiveness will encourage others in your family to do the same and cultivates an environment of understanding and compassion, which are crucial to a stepfamily dynamic.

Forgiving yourself will enable you to approach your relationships with a healthier mindset.

Navigating the complexities of a stepfamily can be challenging, but forgiving yourself will help towards a positive and transparent family space where you demonstrate the importance of being kind to yourself. Let go of any guilt you may be experiencing and move forward, knowing that 'if the Son sets you free, you will be free indeed' (John 8:36). We no longer have to pay the penalty for our sin. Through Christ we have eternal life and a new nature. Guilt is not something we need to embrace, and neither is the shame of past mistakes.

Another one of the enemy's schemes is to encourage us to look back at some of the difficult moments of our past – or to send people our way who will delight in reminding us of those moments. The good news is that you can mark 'return to sender' on all those negative thoughts. Your heavenly Father has taken your sins as far from you 'as the east is from the west' (Psalm 103:12), so forgive yourself.

Enjoy your wonderful new family and life. No regrets. As you consistently practise replacing negative thoughts with positive ones, it will become easier.

Stepping stones

- **Surround yourself with friends** who will celebrate your new life.

- **Place clear boundaries** if the relationship with former spouses is not amicable. Think about how much contact you really need. If your children are older, it's possible that contact can be minimal, particularly if conversations can easily become hurtful and triggering.

- **Pray, and find scripture that you can focus on** to remind yourself of how loved you are and the fact that you are forgiven.

- **Be honest with your spouse.** Let them know what you're going through so you can share that burden together. This will help to prevent misunderstandings and enable you to develop a deeper connection over time.

44

Guilt

**Therefore, if anyone is in Christ, the new creation has come:
the old has gone, the new is here!**
2 CORINTHIANS 5:17

We no longer have to live in regret or suffer consequences for our past. Children can feel guilty about enjoying the new family God has given them. Adults can overcompensate by trying too hard with stepchildren and stepsiblings. We can be overly eager to please, rather than discipline through love as you would with biological children. Trying too hard to make everyone happy will just lead to exhaustion. I remember our first big family holiday; I was determined to ensure everyone had a great time and spent weeks organising the perfect itinerary. In my head it had to be perfect, and I wanted my stepchildren to love it.

They did and we had a great time, but I was run ragged trying to please everyone. My biological children and stepchildren are completely different ages, so it was always going to be a challenge finding activities we could all do together.

My husband took the pressure off afterwards by gently saying that it was fine, that we didn't have to all go away all the time, and that I should just ask the kids what they want to do.

I was busy feeling guilty about half of us going off and having an amazing time while leaving my stepchildren behind. However, we don't need to add our guilt to the price Jesus already paid for us on the cross; his sacrifice was more than enough.

I was trying to control the narrative in terms of being inclusive. A big family holiday is great, but what is God saying for your family? Positive memories can be created anywhere and via many different routes; a simple board game can do wonders to create fun memories. (Pick the right one – maybe not Monopoly if your family, like mine, is super-competitive!)

The point here is that we don't need to engineer grand events to force a bonding process. Bonding takes faith, patience, and love. It's a journey, and your consistency in terms of your character and how you behave will speak volumes. Always remember: love never fails, and guilt will not accomplish anything.

Stepping stones

- **It is a trick of the enemy to constantly remind us of how far we have to go,** as opposed to focusing on the progress we have made.

- **Those who have accepted Jesus Christ as their personal Lord and Saviour are freed from guilt.** The freedom is a result of Jesus' sacrificial death and resurrection, which offers forgiveness and reconciliation with God. It is not something we have to work for.

- **Embrace the idea that in Christ we have a fresh start** and always choose grace over guilt.

- **If you're struggling with guilt today, memorise this:**

  Therefore, there is now no condemnation for those who are in Christ Jesus, because through Christ Jesus the law of the Spirit who gives life has set you free from the law of sin and death.
  ROMANS 8:1–2

45

Hope

Instead of your shame
  you will receive a double portion,
and instead of disgrace
  you will rejoice in your inheritance.
And so you will inherit a double portion in your land,
  and everlasting joy will be yours.

ISAIAH 61:7

The transformative power of grace and redemption is what I love most about stepfamilies. At their heart, our families offer hope. Your union is an illustration of the fact that out of loss, blessing and honour can flow. Isaiah 61:7 presents us with a beautiful promise.

There is always the possibility for joy and renewal. God is the master engineer who takes every difficult circumstance and makes it work out for our good. The nation of Israel went through a lot of bad times. They disobeyed God, were captured by foreign nations, and were taken as captives into exile. God wanted to change their situation and honour them in double measure.

God's anger is for a moment, but his favour is for a lifetime. God wanted to restore Israel back to the place where they rightfully belonged, and he wants to do the same for us. He is a restorer; he is true to his word and wants to see full restoration in our lives, so we experience that abundant life and everlasting joy. Walking in joy is about maintaining a close relationship with God and finding peace in his presence – the kind of perfect peace that gives you permission to live and be excited about life.

There are many times in our lives when God uses adversity as the source of our promotion. When the enemy thought he was getting rid of Joseph, God was simply positioning him for the palace (Genesis 37:23–24; 41:39–41). You have been positioned for overwhelming joy and blessing. Expect double for your trouble. Don't look at other couples and compare yourself with them; be courageous in your difference and walk confidently in your uniqueness. Smile and enjoy your life.

Stepping stones

God's justice will always replace past suffering. Take intentional steps to enjoy your life and live in the joy that you have been promised. Here's how:

- **Faith and trust.** Trust in God's plans for your life and believe that he has your best interests at heart.

- **Prayer.** Spend time in prayer and reflection, and allow yourself to connect with God and feel his peace.

- **Gratitude.** Focus on the great things God has done for you and be thankful. This shifts our perspective to the positives, even in challenging times.

- **Service.** Helping others quickly takes our focus off ourselves and can bring much joy and fulfilment.

- **Community.** We were never designed to do life alone. Surround yourself with people who are proud of you and care and celebrate all of who you and your family are.

46

Beauty for ashes

… and provide for those who grieve in Zion –
to bestow on them a crown of beauty
   instead of ashes,
the oil of joy
   instead of mourning,
and a garment of praise
   instead of a spirit of despair.
They will be called oaks of righteousness,
   a planting of the Lord
   for the display of his splendour.

ISAIAH 61:3

God wants to provide for those who grieve. He wants to give them a crown of beauty instead of ashes, the oil of gladness instead of mourning, and a garment of praise instead of a spirit of despair. And, he has already done it; you just need to receive it.

It is important to understand that we are called not because of anything we are or have done; rather, we are called simply because of the fact that the Spirit of the Lord is upon us – he has anointed us. It's not about us; it's all about him. No further explanation is needed. He has given us beauty for ashes and that is a work of the Spirit. God said it, that settles it. We are simply to study his word, declare it, and apply it to our daily lives. The more we spend time with God, the more his power and goodness become evident in our lives. It is by being in his presence that we become nurtured, established, and crowned with a beautiful headdress.

The oil of joy is a great image. Oil does not come off easily. It shines and leaves anything it touches with a glow. God's oil of joy leaves us with an aura and a presence we carry that cannot be explained, yet causes us to stand out.

As we are busy doing God's business, our heavenly Father, who neither slumbers nor sleeps (Psalm 121:4), is busy minding ours. And, before we know it, we are 'oaks of righteousness', strong in Christ and immovable – the 'planting of the Lord' that he might be glorified.

Stepping stones

- **Remember that God has called you and anointed you for this purpose** and that the opinions and judgement of others are irrelevant in this kingdom equation.

- **You do not have to suffer at the hands of people's judgement.** Don't let the enemy lie to you and steal your future.

- **Walk in your glow; wear your crown with confidence** as a king or queen. Crowns are meant for royalty, and that is exactly what you are as a child of God.

- **Your race is yours to run and the assignment God has given you is yours**; only you can fully understand it. You're not looking for approval from others – you are looking to Jesus, the author and finisher of your faith.

47

Discretion and wisdom

**Discretion will protect you,
and understanding will guard you.**
PROVERBS 2:11

Courage begins again. It bypasses fear and forges a fresh path. When God brings us into something new – whether a restored marriage, a second chance at love, or healing after loss – we need the skills to keep what he has given us. It is important that we don't carry trauma receipts from one relationship to the next. As the Bible encourages us: 'Forget the former things; do not dwell on the past... I am doing a new thing! Now it springs up; do you not perceive it? I am making a way in the wilderness and streams in the wasteland' (Isaiah 43:18–19). Stand on that word; you don't have to fear that past pain will repeat itself.

Discretion and wisdom are the tools God gives us to guard what he has entrusted to us. If our past experiences offer lessons, we can gently learn from them without fear, allowing them to help build a stronger future.

The enemy seeks to stir division where God has ordained restoration, but wisdom teaches us to respond differently. Not every hurt needs revisiting; not every frustration should be spoken aloud. Discretion protects rather than provokes; it heals instead of reopening wounds.

To preserve our families, wisdom reminds us to be careful with our emotions – choosing grace over reaction, patience over impulse, and understanding over judgement. It urges us to value peace over pride and to seek unity over conflict. When we have gone through really tough times, our human nature can cause us to jump to conclusions that signpost to past hurts. I once knew someone who lost their spouse to illness. God gifted them with a new family a few years later, and the new spouse also became ill. Fear began to whisper that history was repeating itself. That couple chose to silence those thoughts and stand on God's promises. Instead of dwelling on what happened before, they fixed their eyes on the God who holds tomorrow. While we cannot predict the future, we can trust the one who governs it.

God has given us beauty for ashes, a fresh opportunity for love and trust. A home without discretion is vulnerable to division, a home guided by wisdom stands strong against future storms.

Stepping stones:

- **Sit down as a couple and reflect on how far you've come** and affirm one another.

- **Love isn't easy to find.** Many people spend their whole lives searching for it. Remember that when the temptation not to resolve issues surfaces. Remember that what you have is an answer to prayer.

- **Build your friendship as a couple.** For example, go on date nights or watch movies together. If you're truly friends, your arguments will decrease, and when you are not speaking you will miss one another.

- **Prayer:** *Lord, in a world where so many people are looking for love, thank you for the gift of family. Give us the wisdom to walk in discretion, so our love for each other will flourish. Protect and preserve us as we do our best to walk uprightly before you.*

Peter and Alison's story

Peter and Alison have been married for eleven years. They met following the sudden loss of Peter's first wife of 25 years. Between them they have seven children: Peter has five from his first marriage, and Alison has twin teenagers. They describe their union as an exciting, God-ordained prophetic journey. Fourteen people gave their life to Christ at their wedding.

Peter says:

> We soaked our marriage in prayer prior to the big day, so there haven't really been many challenges. We introduced both sets of children to each other over a series of dinners beforehand. They are all strong Christians, and understood and were at peace in terms of the new chapter ahead.
>
> Our children were mostly teenagers, bar one who was the baby of the family. Alison has identical twins who were born the same year and the same month as my twins. What was important was to help all the children to see and understand the different giftings and talents they all had, and what they have in common. This helped them to bond quickly as they could see how God had brought them together to help advance and nourish their lives.
>
> It's important to put yourself second in public and first in private and be attentive listeners so the children get the attention they need. You also must show solidarity, be tight, and leave no room for the children to come between you.

Alison continues:

> If one of the children is going through something, Peter will call me and give me a heads up before I come home so I know what I am walking into. Together we have worked out what each

person's strengths and weaknesses are, so all the children can support one another and know that the gifts we have within our family are for everyone.

We can't emphasise enough the importance of prayer, sharing your experiences and what you're going through, along with being humble.

It's also important that churches embrace all families and have a family mediator who can professionally and spiritually support families who may have more complex dynamics to work through, as well as traditional families.

Alison and Peter's top tips

- **Having a strong marriage** will immediately help children to feel safe and secure: work on your marriage.

- **If you're already both bringing children into your union**, it's best to discuss prior to marriage if you want to have more children together and be clear on both sides.

- **It's best to allow children to find their way,** otherwise they are going to fight you. They will come round; prayer will take care of them. Some children may be waiting for a reason to dislike you. Remember, they have had no choice in the new family setup they are in; they didn't get a say.

- **It will not be easy at first, with different parenting styles to get used to.** If you go in knowing the first few years may be hard, it will be easier for you when the challenges do come.

- **Respect and being sensitive are important.** If you're married to someone who lost their first spouse, be sensitive around any key dates that may trigger difficult memories for them and the children who have lost a parent.

- **A key scripture** that really helped us was Philippians 1:6: 'Being confident of this, that he who began a good work in you will carry it on to completion until the day of Christ Jesus.' We also like the phrase 'And God said', which appears for the first time in Genesis in the creation narrative. Simply put, if he hasn't said it, don't do it.

Humility and grief

48

Grief, loss, and your home

God sets the lonely in families,
he leads out the prisoners with singing;
but the rebellious live in a sun-scorched land.
PSALM 68:6

I stood on this verse of scripture for years before I met my husband. A resilient and loving family unit is the heart of God for us all, whatever that looks like. His will is not for us to be lonely or feel desolate; he will provide a home for us that we can dwell in.

Every Christmas my children like to look at all the lights on the houses and choose their favourites. There is a road close to our home where the houses are arrayed with stunning Christmas light displays. The children are always excited by these displays and want us to do similar. Our constant message to them is always: we will do what we can, but always remember a house is not a home.

I believe that when the Bible talks about God providing us with homes to dwell in and placing us in families, it means a safe space where we can thrive, not an environment where we remain a prisoner to our past hurt. He sets the lonely in families where love and growth can take place. He has given you a new home where you can deal with feelings of loss at the same time as embracing the new.

Parents may have healed from the loss of a former spouse and started afresh (or they may not have!), but children may take a lot longer and will be triggered at different points in a new family setting. Memories relating to previous relationship(s) may return from time to time; don't feel guilty. It's important to acknowledge what you're feeling and to speak openly about it and then move at a pace that is comfortable for everyone.

It's essential to create a supportive environment where each member of your family feels safe to express their grief and loss without judgement.

Stepping stones

- **Pray daily as an individual and as a family.** If you are not able to pray as a family, then just pray yourself. Seek comfort and strength from God's unconditional love towards you.

- **Remember that the healing journey following bereavement, separation, or divorce takes time** and is different for us all. Strengthened by your love for one another, take one step at a time, and move forward together.

- **Don't isolate yourself and deal with grief alone.** Turn what you're going through into a shared experience and use it to strengthen your relationship.

- **The Bible says that the strength of God is made perfect in our weakness (see 2 Corinthians 12:9).** This means we can go to God and draw from his divine supply of strength, as he works with our weakness.

49

Grief and retraining your brain

'Forget the former things;
   do not dwell on the past.
See, I am doing a new thing!
   Now it springs up; do you not perceive it?
I am making a way in the wilderness
   and streams in the wasteland.'
ISAIAH 43:18–19

Picture this: after 25 years of marriage, you suddenly lose your spouse. It's a reality no one wants to face, yet it happens. Now imagine moving forward, remarrying, and accidentally calling your new spouse by your first spouse's name – twice. Catastrophic, you might think. But with thoughtful preparation and wise counselling early in the new marriage, these challenges can be anticipated and navigated with grace.

Losing a spouse is devastating. The process of retraining the brain to adjust to their absence takes time and patience, and it will require a great deal of support from your new spouse.

The brain forms patterns and habits through repeated actions and experiences. Over time, neural pathways strengthen with repetition. When it comes to a spouse, especially one you've lived with and loved deeply, these pathways are robust due to daily interactions and shared experiences.

The brain is incredibly agile, meaning it can change and adapt. This neuroplasticity allows it to form new connections and pathways. Over time, with conscious effort and changes in behaviour, the brain can form new associations and reduce the frequency of involuntary recalls of the lost spouse's name. (See **verywellmind.com/ what-is-brain-plasticity-2794886**.)

Healing from loss is a gradual process, and if God has chosen you to be the spouse to someone who lost their first wife or husband, that is an incredible honour. It means you already have the qualities of patience and sensitivity to support them. Remember they love and have chosen you and entrusted you with their children. And God has given you everything you need that pertains to life and Godliness. Together, you've got this!

Stepping stones

Some practical tips for supporting a spouse who lost their first husband or wife:

- **Use visual and auditory cues.** Surrounding yourself with new visual and auditory cues can help. For instance, changing the decor, moving furniture, or even listening to different music can provide subtle reminders that life is moving forward.

- **Be honest at the beginning.** The spouse who has been through the grieving process must be realistic and honest in their new marriage that from time to time there may be triggers: birthdays, certain experiences, or health conditions may trigger difficult memories. If you're married to someone who lost their first spouse, ask God to help you with any insecurities. Pray and help with visual and auditory cues.

- **Use cognitive behavioural techniques.** Techniques like cognitive restructuring can help you change the way you think about certain triggers. This might involve working with a therapist to identify and alter triggering thought patterns.

- **Create new routines.** Establishing new routines can help your brain adapt. Whether it's changing your daily habits or finding new hobbies, these changes can gradually shift your focus.

50

Above all powers

For in him all things were created: things in heaven and on earth, visible and invisible, whether thrones or powers or rulers or authorities; all things have been created through him and for him.
COLOSSIANS 1:16

There can be some incredibly difficult challenges in stepfamilies. Opposition can arise from those who resist or doubt our success. Everything can feel fragile, especially early on, it's easy to feel like you're under constant attack, even when both adults and children are trying so hard. God cares about details. In Colossians, he makes it clear that the highest thrones and authorities were established by him.

On my wedding day, I remember walking round the tables thanking the guests for coming. I approached one table, and a guest warmly said, 'Congratulations. I hope it works.' I remember the face and the comment like it was yesterday. Even on my wedding day, I felt the whisper of failure, before we had even begun.

God is aware of everything. He is not shocked by what we go through, and nothing takes him by surprise. In him all things were created: what we can see and what we can't see. He is the ultimate power. He is above everything: every kingdom, every situation and circumstance, the silent systems that decide they're going to threaten the promise in our hearts. Every mountain and every valley – he stands above it all. Nothing can stand against the governance of God.

Again, you have decided to start afresh. The devil may have rejoiced at your previous circumstance, thinking your story was finished, but what he counted as defeat, God has turned into testimony. In God's hands, endings become new beginnings.

He is high and lifted up. Nothing escapes his attention, and nothing happens without his permission. The Bible says that the Lord sits in heaven and laughs as the kings of the earth and the rulers plot and set themselves against the Lord and his anointed (see Psalm 2:1–4); he holds them in derision. In other words, they are a laughingstock to God – they are not to be taken seriously. It is a mistake for human beings to think they can tear down the plans and purposes that God has divinely orchestrated for those who believe in him and live according to his word.

The book of Acts (17:28) says that in him we live and move and have our being. This means that as we move, our steps are ordered by him. His word is a lamp unto our feet and a light unto our path (Psalm 119:105). We can be in the right place at the right time, and live effective, efficient lives.

If we are in him, abiding under the shadow of his almighty hand, he can make us into whatever he planned for us to be. The schemes of our adversaries will never work, and you deserve the future that God has for you.

 ## Stepping stones

- **Remember, your stepfamily is not just a picture of restoration for today;** it is a declaration that God's purposes will carry forward into a legacy of blessings for generations to come. You can expect the enemy to be mad about that.

- **Stop trying to figure things out.** God has promised to fulfil his plans and purpose in your life, and he will. Be still, and see the salvation of the Lord in your life.

- **I never thought I'd be quoting Warren Buffet, but he said:** 'You will continue to suffer if you have an emotional reaction to everything that is said to you. True power is sitting back and observing things with logic. True power is restraint. If words control you, that means everyone else can control you. Breathe and allow things to pass.'

- **When you know God is in control and that everything is in his hands, you don't need to answer every matter,** and you don't need to have all the answers. He has set before you an open door and no one can close it.

51

Get rid of pride

In the year that king Uzziah died I saw also the Lord sitting upon a throne, high and lifted up, and his train filled the temple.
ISAIAH 6:1 (KJV)

King Uzziah's life serves as a reminder of both the potential for greatness and the consequences of pride and disobedience to God. For stepfamilies, this is especially relevant: when pride dies, God can bring healing and unity across a household that once felt divided. Humility allows his presence to fill the home, just as Isaiah saw the temple filled with his glory.

Uzziah started out strong; he sought the Lord and was successful. The Bible says he did what was right in the sight of the Lord, and as long as he sought the Lord, God made him prosperous. His fame spread far and wide. But he did not finish well, and in the end, pride was his downfall.

Uzziah thought he could do anything he wanted to, even in the name of God. He went into the temple and started to offer incense on the altar of incense when this was a strictly forbidden to all except the priests. Essentially, pride had taken over him. He thought he could chart his own course and not suffer any consequences. 'In the year that King Uzziah dies' can be interpreted as 'in the year that pride dies'. The act of disobedience resulted in him being struck with leprosy and living the remainder of his life in isolation.

God is God of divine order. We are not to promote ourselves; promotion comes from him. We can walk in pride and self-promotion to get somewhere, but then we will find ourselves having to struggle to stay there. When God promotes us, he will keep us and sustain us in that place.

God can do his best work with us when we are humble. The degree to which we can be used by him is determined by the degree to which we walk in humility, place everything in his hands, and stop striving.

Stepping stones

- **Never allow pride to enter your heart.** If you recognise it, nip it in the bud quickly.

   Pride goes before destruction,
   a haughty spirit before a fall.
   Better to be lowly in spirit along with the oppressed
   than to share plunder with the proud.
   PROVERBS 16:18–19

- **In stepfamilies, pride may look like** refusing to ask for the help we need, not saying sorry, or being determined to stand our ground.

- **Humility opens the door to healing.** There are few arguments that humility cannot solve.

- **Everything we are, and everything we have is because of God.** In him and through him all things were created.

- **The story of Uzziah is a stark reminder to us all.** You can read it in 2 Chronicles 26.

- **Pride can also be significant barrier to peace in our relationships,** so be quick to say sorry and quick to forgive.

52

Humility and acceptance

Do nothing out of selfish ambition or vain conceit. Rather, in humility value others above yourselves, not looking to your own interests but each of you to the interests of the others.
    In your relationships with one another, have the same mind-set as Christ Jesus.
PHILIPPIANS 2:3–5

In stepfamilies, you come across issues that biological families just don't have to think about. It takes a good dose of humility to thrive in our beautiful yet complex world. Whether you're new stepparents or veterans, at some point we will say things we shouldn't, read more into a situation than there is, and react first and think later without knowing the full facts. Humility will help hugely. It will reduce the amount of friction in your marriage and family.

To be meek and modest in our temperament isn't weakness; it is the recognition of the fact that God governs our lives. It is also helpful to be honest and accept that we don't always have the answers and simply figuring things out together can actually be fun if you allow it to be.

Embracing each other's pasts, including former relationships with ex-spouses and memories shared, is essential. It doesn't just take humility; it's also about acceptance and grace. It will also help us understand that the experiences and feelings of others are just as valid as our own. For example, a stepparent walking in humility can ease the transition by acknowledging they are not there to replace a biological parent but to provide additional love and support. Suddenly the fears and anxieties of younger, or even older children, are allayed.

Our journeys together do not start out as blended, but as we run after the present, while humbly accepting the history that each person brings to this new union, the knitting together and those cords of love that can never be broken are formed. This includes welcoming stepparents, step siblings, and grandchildren with grace, no matter what age they are.

Stepping stones

- **Humility releases God's grace** to us in the many difficult areas of life we face.

- **There are no relationship problems that humility cannot solve,** providing each party is connected to God – or willing to follow biblical principles.

- **God makes it clear that we are ineffective if we are not being loving at all times.** And, when we read what the behaviour of love looks like, it becomes obvious via multiple verses of scripture that humility is at the heart of love.

- **Some key verses:**

  Be completely humble and gentle; be patient, bearing with one another in love.
  EPHESIANS 4:2

  Bear with each other and forgive one another if any of you has a grievance against someone. Forgive as the Lord forgave you.
  COLOSSIANS 3:13

  He gives us more grace. That is why Scripture says: 'God opposes the proud but shows favour to the humble.'
  JAMES 4:6

53

The spirit of offence

Above all else, guard your heart,
for everything you do flows from it.
PROVERBS 4:23

Offence will steal from you. It can turn into bitterness, resentment, and unforgiveness if you don't deal with it straight away. And, before you know it, your home is in turmoil and sometimes you can't even remember what the original thing was that you were offended about. In relationships, especially in stepfamilies, it's usually the small things that accumulate and then become major issues. Deal with them immediately.

Many people never fulfil their purpose or become all God desires them to be simply because they got offended. It becomes a hindrance to them being able to think clearly, and they don't progress.

This is why we must guard our hearts – above all else. Scripture places a strong emphasis on the heart as a source of good or evil in relation to our behaviour.

Jesus said: 'The good person out of the good treasure of his heart pro-duces good, and the evil person out of his evil treasure produces evil, for out of the abundance of the heart his mouth speaks' (Luke 6:45, ESV). Our hearts will produce actions that reflect its true condition. What are you being influenced by? What are you watching, reading, or listening to? Fill your heart with good things, and it will produce good things.

We can choose to believe the best of people and situations that we find ourselves in. We can choose to give people the benefit of the doubt and focus on the things that we can control and not the things we can't. Diligently guarding our hearts helps us to stay emotionally healthy; it encourages self-awareness and self-care so we can bring the best version of ourselves into our relationships. It is the antidote to offence.

Stepping stones

- **'Above all else' is a major thing to include in a verse of scripture within a book filled with wisdom.** Guarding the heart is above everything because all wickedness and all love proceed from it, both good fruit and bad (Luke 6:45).

- **It is important to set healthy boundaries to ensure negative and harmful influences don't infiltrate our homes.** Limit exposure to negative people or environments.

- **Diligence in our heart will translate to stronger commitment towards making all the relationships in our lives work.** It involves being dedicated to consistently wanting to produce good fruit in our lives.

- **Practise self-reflection.** Regularly take time to think about your actions, thoughts, and emotions. Writing a journal can be good for this. It will help you to process what you're feeling and identify the areas that need attention.

Sarah and Ewan's story

Sarah and Ewan have been together for 45 years. They have two biological children and Ewan has one child from a previous relationship. Early on in their relationship, Sarah often resented being left at home with her stepson when Ewan went to work. Being very young at the time, Sarah didn't know what to do.

She says:

> I tried to be a mum when I didn't need to – this is a lesson that took me a while to learn. Then my mum said to me, 'If the roles were reversed, what would you do?', and that helped.
>
> There were times when I felt taken for granted, but that was also mixed with joy. Slowly I learnt that it wasn't my responsibility to take the role of a parent, rather to build trust and respect.

Ewan agrees:

> I had no nervousness about Sarah's role in my son's life. I never really looked at it as a stepparent scenario; we were a family. When he came to stay with us, he was part of our home. We didn't do anything different. We were consistent in sticking to our regular routine.
>
> Striking the right balance is crucial to ensuring the individual needs of all the children are met. Words are incredibly powerful, and it's wise to avoid using the term 'step' when speaking in front of your stepchildren. You might unintentionally make them feel excluded or inferior, as though they aren't fully part of the family or that things change when they are not there.
>
> They are also processing how they belong, and how they see themselves in the process. It's the child's journey to make, so allow them space to decide how they want to relate to you.

Sarah continues:

> It's family at the end of the day. Family is such a blessing. Today we see all our children grown up and very close, they have each other, and times like Christmas are wonderful. When you see them doing the things that you used to do and continuing family traditions, you feel so proud.
>
> It's vital to remember the Bible tells us that children are a gift from God. That's all children.

Scriptures that were important to us on our journey were:

> Children are a heritage from the Lord,
>   offspring a reward from him.
> PSALM 127:3

> Start children off on the way they should go,
>   and even when they are old they will not turn from it.
> PROVERBS 22:6

Sarah and Ewan's top tips

- **Focus on simply spending time** with your children.

- **We didn't get overly consumed with providing** – men might especially need to hear that. Doing lots of fun stuff to entertain, and working all hours to sustain that lifestyle, could mean being absent and neglecting what is important.

- **When we look back at our memories of raising our children**, and asked them what they enjoyed growing up, the trip to Walt Disney World Resort in Florida didn't feature. Our simple Friday takeaway nights eating Chinese on the floor was a special time all the children remember.

Prayer and the
Holy Spirit

54

Embracing the Holy Spirit

But the Advocate, the Holy Spirit, whom the Father will send in my name, will teach you all things and will remind you of everything I have said to you.
JOHN 14:26

We must never forget the role of the Holy Spirit in our lives. When you embrace the anointing and guidance of the Holy Spirit, you open your family to a path filled with divine support, healing, and love. This journey, though sometimes challenging, can be profoundly enriching with the Holy Spirit's presence. There is a price to pay for those who desire the anointing, and it starts on our knees. No family can be successful and exhibit the abundant life that God has promised us by winging it. As important as it is for us as stepparents to find our tribe and our core community of people we can trust, it's equally important to separate ourselves and pray for our marriages, and for everyone that is a part of our family. We must give ourselves completely to God. I know it's not easy once we have children and stepchildren with multiple activities that demand our time and attention.

We don't need to be religious about our prayer life, but we do need to carve out time each day to spend with God. Then also look for those key opportunities throughout our day when we can check in with him.

I find with my children that when I get up early to pray, one of them will often come in to disturb me. No matter how much I tell them, 'This is mummy's prayer time and, trust me, you need Mamma to have the anointing!', they still come in. Now I leave the house and go walking early in the morning and pray, praise, and worship.

Find the rhythm that works for you and be consistent. The anointing makes the difference, and you will see results in every area of your life.

Stepping stones

- **Surrender each day to God.** And remember: surrendering is a process, not a one-time thing. We have to daily commit ourselves to his service; it's not easy or for the faint-hearted. Surrendering isn't convenient or comfortable. It is what is required if we want to flow in the power of the Holy Spirit's anointing. It is constant and consistent communion with God.

- **You don't have to have been a Christian for years to live a life of complete surrender.** It's simply about a hunger and a passion for more. You simply ask for the grace to show up daily and as you do, God will do the rest. It isn't about enticing words of man's wisdom. It's about a childlike desire to just want more of God.

- **Key verse:**

  For those who are led by the Spirit of God are the children of God.
  ROMANS 8:14

55

The fruit of the Spirit

But the fruit of the Spirit is love, joy, peace, forbearance, kindness, goodness, faithfulness, gentleness and self-control. Against such things there is no law.
GALATIANS 5:22–23

I've learnt to treat the Holy Spirit as a person with feelings, emotions, and desires of his own. In doing this, we can ask him in the morning for direction and anytime when we're feeling unsure about what to do. Even if we know, instinctively, what approach to take to a situation, making a habit of quietly asking 'Is this the right thing to do?' will strengthen your clarity of mind. It does feel a bit odd to start with, but the more you talk to the Holy Spirit, the more familiar you become with hearing that still, small voice. It's about a relationship, not an isolated experience.

You can start by asking for the fruit of his Spirit to be evident in your life. Patience (or forbearance), kindness, gentleness, and self-control are crucial to our being able to relate well with others. This is where you start to ask yourself: *Is it more important to win an argument or to flow in the anointing and maintain fellowship with the Holy Spirit?* The Bible tells us that we can grieve the Holy Spirit, and the more we develop our prayer life, the more sensitive we will become to not wanting to do this.

When you start on this journey of stepparenting, very likely all hell will break lose in your home, work, everywhere, as the enemy starts to try to distract you from your goal of practising the presence of God. Don't compromise; see the temptation to give up for what it is, a distraction.

Stepping stones

- **Prayer and the anointing of God transform men and women** into supernatural people.

- **God cannot entrust his anointing to people who don't pray.** The people who you observe who live powerful lives for Christ will be praying people.

- **We have to be disciplined even when we don't feel like it.** We need to pay the price on our knees. When we do, we will see the results in our homes, in our health, and in our ability to make the right decisions and good choices. We also pave the way for our children to emulate what they see and pass on a powerful legacy to the next generation.

- **Declare this:** *My family have the fruit of the Spirit embedded in our lives, and the light we carry will bring hope to our generation. We will not fail, we will fulfil destiny, we will not be derailed, and we will not be distracted.*

56

Prayer and your home

> **One day Jesus was praying in a certain place. When he finished, one of his disciples said to him, 'Lord, teach us to pray, just as John taught his disciples.'**
> LUKE 11:1

Have you ever been in a prayer meeting where people are verbosely shouting, sweating, and shaking as they cry out to God? There is nothing wrong with this; everyone has their own style. However, prayer isn't about fancy words. We are not trying to impress people with our memory of scripture or spiritual aptitude.

It is, though, important that we pray effectively, with clarity and boldness. Praying in line with the Bible and using scripture when we pray will help us align our prayer lives with what God wants for us. You will also gain strength for your specific family situation as you read the word and have a conversation with him.

The Bible says that we should approach the throne of grace with boldness and confidence to obtain help in our time of need (see Hebrews 4:16). Have a set of scriptures that you can use to pray over your family declaring the change you want to see. All the material you need is in the Bible. You will grow in your ability to pray as you commit or re-commit to the fun journey of reading and praying.

Here are some verses that relate to the fruit of the Spirit, that is, 'love, joy, peace, forbearance, kindness, goodness, faithfulness, gentleness and self-control (Galatians 5:22–23):

Love is patient, love is kind. It does not envy, it does not boast, it is not proud. It does not dishonour others, it is not self-seeking, it is not easily angered, it keeps no record of wrongs… It always protects, always trusts, always hopes, always perseveres.
1 CORINTHIANS 13:4–7

Rejoice in the Lord always. I will say it again: rejoice!
PHILIPPIANS 4:4

Let the peace of Christ rule in your hearts, since as members of one body you were called to peace. And be thankful.
COLOSSIANS 3:15

Be completely humble and gentle; be patient, bearing with one another in love.
EPHESIANS 4:2

Be kind and compassionate to one another, forgiving each other, just as in Christ God forgave you.
EPHESIANS 4:32

Therefore, as we have opportunity, let us do good to all people, especially to those who belong to the family of believers.
GALATIANS 6:10

Let love and faithfulness never leave you;
    bind them round your neck,
    write them on the tablet of your heart.
PROVERBS 3:3

Let your gentleness be evident to all. The Lord is near.
PHILIPPIANS 4:5

For the Spirit God gave us does not make us timid, but gives us power, love and self-discipline.
2 TIMOTHY 1:7

 **Stepping stones**

- **If you don't know how to pray, ask the Holy Spirit to help you.** Then pick two or three scriptures that relate to your prayer point and incorporate them into your daily prayer time.

- **Ideally, it's good to pray as a family.** If this isn't always possible, encourage personal prayer as well as family prayer time. Establish prayer as a non-negotiable part of your lives so you create a strong spiritual foundation in your home.

- **Pray this:** *Heavenly Father, teach us how to pray and how to build a strong spiritual foundation in our homes and help us to be consistent in doing this regularly. Let the peace of Christ rule our hearts and home. Help us to be kind and compassionate to one another, forgiving one another as Christ forgave us. Give us cause to rejoice always and let your joy be seen in our lives.*

57

Laziness vs discipline

No discipline seems pleasant at the time, but painful. Later on, however, it produces a harvest of righteousness and peace for those who have been trained by it.
HEBREWS 12:11

Successful people are not lazy; it's as simple as that. If we want to see the power of God in our homes, we have to drag ourselves out of bed and be disciplined and pray. This may sound repetitive, but we are human. Often, we get ourselves into a good routine for a couple of months, and then we fall off track, and then we get back on track, and we go back and forth. Procrastination rears its ugly head, or life just gets busy. Generally, life gets busy!

Here's the thing that I've found: if the enemy can't stop us from doing something great, he will stop us from doing something great consistently. Progress happens with discipline, commitment, and consistency. We will see significant results if we take small steps repeatedly over time. We will get the breakthrough we desire to see in our lives.

We don't get breakthrough by pursing breakthroughs; we get them by making consistent daily changes to our attitudes, approaches, and lifestyle. Eventually our consistency will compound and, without even realising it, that thing we were praying for daily has shifted. Suddenly, you're relating skilfully with your stepchildren. Suddenly, you're not receiving difficult messages from the biological parent. Suddenly, you're not having arguments with your spouse over blending the different sets of children in your home. The compound effect of consistent and persistent prayer and anointing happened. You can't change your spiritual state overnight, but you can change your spiritual discipline today.

Stepping stones

- **Read *The Compound Effect* by Darren Hardy.** The core of the book contains a principle that small, consistent actions or changes, repeated over time, can lead to significant and exponential results. It's a great book to help us lead disciplined lives.

- **On discipline:**

  Therefore, my dear brothers and sisters, stand firm. Let nothing move you. Always give yourselves fully to the work of the Lord, because you know that your labour in the Lord is not in vain.
  1 CORINTHIANS 15:58

  Whoever loves discipline loves knowledge,
      but whoever hates correction is stupid.
  PROVERBS 12:1

- **On consistency:**

  Let us not become weary in doing good, for at the proper time we will reap a harvest if we do not give up.
  GALATIANS 6:9

58

Ask God for your dream family

'Ask and it will be given to you; seek and you will find; knock and the door will be opened to you. For everyone who asks receives; the one who seeks finds; and to the one who knocks, the door will be opened.'
MATTHEW 7:7–8

If something is in your heart, it's likely there for a reason. You can have the dream family you've always wished for. Ever watched the TV and seen a perfect-looking family in one of those Hallmark movies with the Christmas decorations perfectly packed on to every available space and fireplace, and the family photos perfectly hung on every wall?

Of course, it's just a movie, and no one has a family or even a house like that! But you may find yourself asking why your family can't be the dream family that you have always had in your heart.

This is the confidence we have in approaching God: that if we ask anything according to his will, he hears us. And if we know that he hears us – whatever we ask – we know that we have what we asked of him.
1 JOHN 5:14–15

Does God want us to have happy homes and thriving families? Of course he does. Is he big enough to do that for us? Of course he is! Our busy lives lead to us sometimes forgetting how big our God is. We start behaving like he is small and that some things are too difficult for him to do. We don't mean to have a poverty mentality, but we do, and we are not clear about what we want. Don't settle for okay when you can have amazing! He asks us to come boldly when we ask. His word states that nothing is too hard for him, and that we can have confidence that he hears our prayers.

There are numerous places in the Bible where God encourages us to ask for things and promises to respond. If God says something once, that is good enough, but if he repeats a principle repeatedly, he is trying to get our attention. This reinforces the message that God is attentive to our requests and is willing to provide for us according to his will and wisdom.

Stepping stone

- **Ask big and dream big for your family.** If you are not where you want to be today, write down exactly where you would like to be in a year's time and speak the word of faith over your marriage and your children. Believe that you can have a peaceful and joyous home, and watch God work. Faith comes by hearing, and hearing by the word (see Romans 10:17). Develop your faith muscles and believe for more.

- **Some verses:**

  'If you believe, you will receive whatever you ask for in prayer.'
  MATTHEW 21:22

  'In that day you will no longer ask me anything. Very truly I tell you, my Father will give you whatever you ask in my name. Until now you have not asked for anything in my name. Ask and you will receive, and your joy will be complete.'
  JOHN 16:23–24

  Now to him who is able to do immeasurably more than all we ask or imagine, according to his power that is at work within us.
  EPHESIANS 3:20

59

Focused, faithful, and fruitful

Let us not become weary in doing good, for at the proper time we will reap a harvest if we do not give up.
GALATIANS 6:9

Blending a family is a journey that requires patience, understanding, and unwavering faith. As you navigate the complexities of stepparenting, remember the words of Proverbs 16:3: 'Commit to the Lord whatever you do, and he will establish your plans.' This verse serves as our foundation, reminding us to remain focused on God's purpose for our families.

The process of blending a family may come with challenges and hardship. There will be moments when misunderstandings arise, and differences seem insurmountable. However, it is in these times that we must remain faithful, trusting in God's promise to guide us through. Galatians 6:9 encourages us to not grow weary in doing the right thing. This verse reassures us that our perseverance and dedication will yield results in due time.

As stepfamilies, for both adults and children, staying focused on what truly matters is essential. Ephesians 4:2–3 reminds us: 'Be completely humble and gentle; be patient, bearing with one another in love. Make every effort to keep the unity of the Spirit through the bond of peace.' By embedding an environment of love, patience, and unity, we create a strong foundation for our families to succeed.

It is through our faithfulness to God's calling that we will see the fruit of our labour. Our efforts to build meaningful relationships, rooted in love and understanding, will not go unnoticed. As we focus on his guidance and remain steadfast in our faith, God will bless our families abundantly.

Embrace the journey of blending your family with a spirit of perseverance and trust in God's plan. Be focused and stay faithful to the principles of your faith. It is only a matter of time before you see his love and grace in every aspect of your lives.

Stepping stones

- **Please remember that absolutely nothing goes unnoticed by our heavenly Father,** and he is not unjust.

- **God's delight is to show us off.** As human parents, we are super proud of our children even though at times they will do the wrong thing. It's common nowadays for parents, when their children make some progress, to share photos of it on social media and celebrate even the smallest victory. If that is what we are like as earthly parents, how much more so is God.

- **God wants us to be successful;** he wants us to experience the beauty-for-ashes life (see Isaiah 61:3).

60

The role of the church in supporting stepfamilies

So we, though many, are one body in Christ, and individually members one of another.
ROMANS 12:5 (ESV)

My husband and I prepared well for our marriage, including doing pre-marital counselling. However, we still weren't ready for the realities of our home. Early on, I focused on how I could ensure my stepchildren felt secure in their new family space, but what I didn't know was that I was pregnant with my honeymoon baby a few months after getting married. Another one came along not too long after, so that in the space of three years, our children grew from two to four. As a stepparent, you're excited about the journey of getting to know your partner's children, but there can be many flies in the ointment, too, such as dealing with your new partner's ex-spouse, who has the potential to turn your whole world upside down in a second.

The church has a unique and vital role in ministering to our families. We are a growing demographic that deserves to be seen and supported. We feel our way through the fog of intricate issues, including blending traditions, finances, managing past relationships, and figuring out a new and beautiful normal. While these challenges can feel isolating, the body of Christ is called to walk alongside us in love and understanding.

Church ministries can prioritise intentional efforts to engage step-families from the outset of their journey. Premarital and family counselling tailored specifically for remarried couples and their children can help establish strong foundations and address potential struggles.

Dedicated support groups for stepfamilies provide spaces for honest conversation, encouragement, and shared experiences. These groups can build connections and remind families that they are not alone.

As stepfamilies grow, the church can design teaching materials and sermon series that speak directly to their unique experiences. Lessons on forgiveness, grace, and unity can be crafted to meet our needs. Testimonies from stepfamilies in church services and outreach events will celebrate stepfamily stories and affirm our place in the community, so we don't feel 'othered'.

Family-oriented activities, such as retreats or workshops, should accommodate the diversity of families within the church. By creating inclusive spaces, where every member feels valued, church communities can go further in reflecting the fullness of Christ's love.

Stepping stones

- **Stepfamilies should never feel that church activities or family ministry fail to recognise their experiences.**

- **Through targeted meaningful ministry**, the church can stand as a beacon of hope, reminding stepfamilies of our worth and integral role in the body of Christ.

- **Together, we can help our church families to understand the redemptive power in stepfamilies.**

- **Few churches have a stepfamily ministry**, but you can change this. Approach your church leaders and ask if you can hold a support event for the stepfamilies in your church or even for the stepfamilies that are in the community that your church is located in. This also has the potential to become a powerful outreach tool.

God's promises to the courageous stepfamily

He who was seated on the throne said, 'I am making everything new! Then he said, write this down, for these words are trustworthy and true.'
REVELATION 21:5

He heals the broken-hearted
and binds up their wounds.
PSALM 147:3

The Lord himself goes before you and will be with you; he will never leave you nor forsake you. Do not be afraid; do not be discouraged.
DEUTERONOMY 31:8

The Spirit of the Sovereign Lord is on me,
because the Lord has anointed me
to proclaim good news to the poor.
He has sent me to bind up the broken-hearted,
to proclaim freedom for the captives
and release from darkness for the prisoners.
ISAIAH 61:1

God sets the lonely in families,
he leads out the prisoners with singing;
but the rebellious live is a sun-scorched land.
PSALM 68:6

'I will restore you to health
   and heal your wounds,'
      declares the Lord.
JEREMIAH 30:17

'I will give you a new heart and put a new spirit in you; I will remove from you your heart of stone and give you a heart of flesh.'
EZEKIEL 36:26

'I will repay you for the years the locusts have eaten.'
JOEL 2:25

But he said to me, 'My grace is sufficient for you, for my power is made perfect in weakness.' Therefore, I will boast all the more gladly about my weaknesses, so that Christ's power may rest on me.
2 CORINTHIANS 12:9

Now to him who is able to do immeasurably more than all we ask or imagine according to the power that is at work within us.
EPHESIANS 3:20

Therefore confess your sins to each other and pray for each other so that you may be healed. The prayer of a righteous person is powerful and effective.
JAMES 5:16

Humble yourselves, therefore, under God's mighty hand, that he may lift you up in due time. Cast all your anxiety on him because he cares for you.
1 PETER 5:6–7

A passage that refers to priorities and focusing on what truly matters:

> 'Martha, Martha,' the Lord answered, 'you are worried and upset about many things, but few things are needed – or indeed only one. Mary has chosen what is better, and it will not be taken away from her.'
> LUKE 10:41–42

An encouraging reminder that no matter what, God is faithful to complete what he begun in your lives:

> Being confident of this, that he who began a good work in you will carry it on to completion until the day of Christ Jesus.
> PHILIPPIANS 1:6

ANNA HAWKEN

BEING GOD'S CHILD

A PARENT'S GUIDE

Ten things you can learn from your kids

Includes sessions for small groups

God makes us the most unbelievable offer – to be our parent. Yes, even when we're all grown up and have children of our own! But many of us don't live experiencing the connection, guidance and support that's on offer. Why? Because we've forgotten how to be a child. In this easy-to-read guide, Anna Hawken explores ten different ways to rediscover our 'child side'. She uses the living, breathing examples of the children in our lives to inspire and challenge us, by looking at things that we sometimes struggle with but they are great at.

Being God's Child: A Parent's Guide
Ten things you can learn from your kids
Anna Hawken
978 1 80039 198 7 £6.99

brfresources.org.uk

Collecting all the wisdom of titles previously published as *Parenting Children for a Life of Faith*, *Parenting Children for a Life of Purpose*, and *Parenting Children for a Life of Confidence*. This book provides inspiration and wisdom for nurturing children into the reality of God's presence and love, equipping them to access him themselves and encouraging them to grow in a two-way relationship with him that will last a lifetime.

Parenting Children for a Life of Faith: Omnibus Edition
Helping children meet and know God
Rachel Turner
978 0 85746 694 5 £12.99

brfresources.org.uk

Ministries

Inspiring people of all ages to grow in Christian faith

BRF Ministries is the home of Anna Chaplaincy, BRF Resources, Messy Church and Parenting for Faith

As a charity, our work would not be possible without fundraising and gifts in wills.
To find out more and to donate,
visit brf.org.uk/give or call +44 (0)1865 319700